BALINESE
GAMELAN
MUSIC

Balinese gongs carried in procession.

BALINESE GAMELAN MUSIC

By Michael Tenzer

TUTTLE Publishing

Tokyo | Rutland, Vermont | Singapore

Published by Tuttle Publishing, an imprint of Periplus Editions (HK) Ltd.

www.tuttlepublishing.com

ISBN 978-0-8048-4186-3
(previously published as Balinese Music, isbn 978-962-593-169-2)

ILLUSTRATIONS:
I Madé Moja

PHOTOGRAPHS:
Rio Helmi: pages 113, 121, color inserts pages iv, vi–vii, viii (both photos), ix, x–xi, xii, xiii
(bottom left and right), xiv (both photos), xvi (top)
Tom Ballinger: pages 2, 14, 32, 51, 52, 53, 57, 108, 118, 138, 141, color inserts pages i, xiii
(top), xv
K. Prasetya: pages 127, 130
Kal Muller: pages 61, color inserts page v
Eric Oey: pages 34, color inserts page xvi (bottom)
Hans Höfer: color inserts pages ii–iii
Mike Hosken: page 87
Jeannette Hlavach: page 6
Greg MacKinnon: page 12
Michael Tenzer: pages 133, 157

Distributed by:

North America, Latin America & Europe
Tuttle Publishing
364 Innovation Drive
North Clarendon, VT 05759-9436 U.S.A.
Tel: 1 (802) 773-8930
Fax: 1 (802) 773-6993
info@tuttlepublishing.com
www.tuttlepublishing.com

Asia Pacific
Berkeley Books Pte. Ltd.
61 Tai Seng Avenue, #02-12
Singapore 534167
Tel: (65) 6280-1330
Fax: (65) 6280-6290
inquiries@periplus.com.sg
www.periplus.com

Japan
Tuttle Publishing
Yaekari Building, 3rd Floor
5-4-12 Osaki, Shinagawa-ku
Tokyo 141-0032
Tel: (81) 3 5437-0171
Fax: (81) 3 5437-0755
sales@tuttle.co.jp
www.tuttle.co.jp

Indonesia
PT Java Books Indonesia
Kawasan Industri Pulogadung
Jl. Rawa Gelam IV No. 9
Jakarta 13930
Tel: (62) 21 4682-1088
Fax: (62) 21 461-0206
crm@periplus.co.id
www.periplus.co.id

Third edition
15 14 13 12 11   1103TP
8 7 6 5 4 3 2 1

Printed in Singapore

TUTTLE PUBLISHING® is a registered trademark of Tuttle Publishing, a division of
Periplus Editions (HK) Ltd.

Contents

PREFACE TO THE THIRD EDITION 7

PREFACE TO THE FIRST EDITION 9

CHAPTER 1: **An Introduction to Balinese Music**...................................13

CHAPTER 2: **A Brief History of the Music Through the Late Twentieth Century** 22

CHAPTER 3: **The Construction and Tuning of Instruments**..................33

CHAPTER 4: **Basic Principles of Gamelan Music**......................................47

CHAPTER 5: **The Music for the Baris Dance** 67

CHAPTER 6: **Ensembles and Repertoire**...84

CHAPTER 7: **Music in Balinese Society**...114

CHAPTER 8: **Three Generations of Balinese Musicians**........................125

CHAPTER 9: **Getting Involved**..136

CHAPTER 10: **Balinese Music Since 1990**...145

APPENDIX...161

FURTHER READING..162

RECORDINGS OF BALINESE MUSIC...168

GLOSSARY...171

INDEX 179

CONTENTS OF THE COMPACT DISC..188

The *ceng-ceng* player in the famous *gamelan gong kebyar* from Pindha village.

Preface to the Third Edition

I wrote the first nine chapters of this book in Bali during April and May of 1989, in a lined composition notebook, with a ball-point pen in longhand, on the porch of a rented *pondok* (bamboo-and-thatch cabin). This was at the peaceful compound of my friend Ketut Madra, a painter living at the southern end of Peliatan village. Madra's sweetness and warm conversation have sheltered me since my first trip to Bali in 1977. While writing I was refreshed by the surrounding vista of lush gardens and breeze-kissed ricefields, the pulsing vocal polyrhythms of canine, bovine, birds caged and free, porcine, cricket, frog, and fowl, and the chopping, scraping and conversation of woodworkers and brickmakers in a compound next door. Later, across the Pacific, I typed the manuscript into my then-new 20K hard disk Mac SE, and snail-mailed it to the publisher on blue-shelled floppies.

These lines are being written on the same porch, twenty-one years later, now on a laptop. The pondok is faded and worn, and the ricefields have receded behind multi-story buildings, thus diminishing much of the creature chorus. Except for a few hours before dawn, the rumbling traffic noise out on the main road underpins what is left of it. Elsewhere in the crowded Peliatan-Ubud area, at homestays and hotels more upscale than humble Madra's, with landscaping, air conditioned rooms, staff, and fountains, a version of 1989 Bali (or earlier) can still be had, but it is something of a fantasy created for visitors. Readers ought to know, though, that no disparagement is intended when I speak of the "packaged" Bali, for it is as real as any other facet of the island. A short distance off the main commercial and tourist routes, for now, one can still avoid the commodification.

This book has always been addressed to visitors, plus admirers and would-be visitors, who want to understand Bali's magnificent, endlessly satisfying music, and through it some aspects of the Balinese. Many important changes have affected Bali since 1989, and *gamelan* music is now made in ever-multiplying musical varieties and contexts in Bali and around the world. I describe some of these in a new final chapter. As for the rest of the book, there was no need to more than lightly edit and update it. Though all of the musicians portrayed have obviously moved on, and in some cases passed away, the legacy of their contributions is fully alive and revered. It is important to preserve it for a general readership here. Naturally there has been a generational changing of the guard, and some of the major new voices are introduced in Chapter Ten.

In the book's original preface I thanked, and would now like to thank again, the musicians of Gamelan Sekar Jaya in California. Thirty-one years on from its 1979 founding it is still the flagship of Balinese music and dance in the wider world, and a household name in Bali. But my life and gamelan hands took me elsewhere. Now my thanks extend to the members of Gamelan Jagat Anyar of New Haven, Connecticut, and Gamelan Gita Asmara of Vancouver, plus groups at the Conservatoires of Rueil-Malmaison and Creteil in Paris. The formidable young musician-composer Wayan Sudirana and his wife, dancer Putu Widiantini, are currently our resident directors in Vancouver. If they are any indication, Balinese music and dance are going to be explosively alive for a long time to come.

More than ever the book is for Pam, Molly, and Maya too.

Michael Tenzer,
Peliatan, Bali (and Vancouver, B.C.)

Preface to the First Edition

In 1976, as a young composer in college, not quite out of my teens and with a healthy appetite for aural stimulus, I chanced to overhear an animated conversation between a wonderful jazz pianist whom I knew and another friend. I was just walking by, but caught the phrase "*gamelan* music," preceded by a string of superlatives. The word "gamelan" sparked something in me, even though I had never heard it before. Turning on my heels I headed to the local record store and bought the only gamelan release that I could find—a record of Balinese music on the Nonesuch label—and made for my dorm room. Before taking off my coat I put the disc on the stereo and turned up the volume. I felt my eyes opening very wide and was quickly swept into a state of intense concentration. Within ten minutes I had made a pact with myself to go to Bali and learn how to make the beautiful and challenging sounds that were rushing out of the speakers. (Much later, I learned that my friend had actually been speaking about the Javanese gamelan, which never would have captivated me as the Balinese did. I've always considered my mistake in the record store to be a great stroke of luck.)

A year hence, on my twentieth birthday, I stepped off the ferry from Banyuwangi, in East Java, to find myself staring up at an enormous temple gate in Gilimanuk, in West Bali. It was almost midnight and I had been traveling for three days, including a long stretch of a slow, hot train. I was already delirious from a list of illnesses and but dimly aware that I had to lug my bags onto a bus now rumbling towards me—for a three hour ride to Denpasar. But the night was clear, and I still remember how the gate seemed to welcome me.

I had brought a few letters of introduction and had some contacts. Settling in Peliatan village at the home of the painter Ketut Madra, I began music lessons with Nyoman Sumandhi at the KOKAR High School of Music and Dance. My first studies were the Baris melody, ornamentation, and drumming which is presented here in Chapter Five. Sumandhi entreated me to feel like family, taking me under his wing and all over Bali on the back of his Honda. It was not long before I was having lengthy lessons twice daily. In the six months I was there, my language skills sputtered and finally began to rev. Evenings I composed, borrowing from what my teachers had taught me. My delight in the music quickly earned me many musician friends. Without quite knowing what I would do with them, I bought a set of instruments to bring back to the States.

Arriving in Berkeley, California in the fall of 1979 with my instruments in tow, I began graduate school in Western music. I joined up with my friends Rachel Cooper and the Balinese drummer I Wayan Suweca to found a gamelan organization. We modeled ourselves on the community-based musical clubs of Bali, and attracted many enthusiastic members. I still marvel at the music's ability to take root so removed from its natural environs. Suweca stayed for two years, but after he went home the group—which he had named Sekar Jaya (Victorious Flower)—continued to support residencies for a string of Balinese musicians and dancers. One thing had led to another. I had succeeded in surrounding myself with Balinese music as if it were a cocoon, both at home and in Bali. I have been back to Indonesia for more many times since.

My years of experience with this music have turned me into an enthusiastic disseminator, in reverence of this artistic tradition and the people and culture that possess it. No music in the world can corner the market on beauty, sophistication, subtlety or any other aesthetic identity, but Balinese music does possess a singular mix of orchestral complexity and a strong commitment to group interaction that makes it inspirational. Balinese gamelan rehearse to perfect their music more than any other large ensembles in the world. The process with which the music is made creates a unique personal bond between members of the group, which is precisely what playing music should be all about.

There are so many Balinese teachers and friends who I want to thank and write about here, all of whom have enriched me and inspired me, but there is only room to list their names. They include Ni Ketut Arini Alit, Ketut Gdé Asnawa, I Wayan Gama Astawa, I Komang Astita, I Madé Bandem, Ni Luh Swasthi Bandem, Dewa Nyoman Batuan, I Wayan Beratha, I Madé Canderi, I Nyoman Catra, I Madé Demong, I Wayan Dibia, I Madé Gableran, I

Wayan Gandera, I Ketut Gantas, I Madé Grindem, Anak Agung Putu Griya, I Madé Griya, Cokorda Alit Hendrawan, I Wayan Jebeg, I Madé Jimat, Ni Wayan Konderi, I Wayan Konolan, I Ketut Kumpul, Desak Madé Laksmi, Ni Putu Lastini, I Madé Lebah, I Wayan Loceng, I Gusti Lumbung, I Ketut Madra, Anak Agung Gdé Mandera, Gdé Manik, Cokorda Mas, Ida Bagus Raka Negara, I Gusti Ngurah Panji, I Wayan Pogog, I Wayan Rai, Ida Bagus Aji Madé Regog, I Nyoman Rembang, I Ketut Rintig, Ni Wayan Roni, Anak Agung Raka Saba, I Wayan Sinti, Ni Gusti Ayu Srinatih, I Wayan Sujana, I Nyoman Sumandhi, Ni Ketut Suryatini, I Madé Suta, I Wayan Suweca, I Ketut Tama, I Wayan Tembres, I Ketut Tutur, Nanik Wenten, I Nyoman Wenten, I Nyoman Windha, I Wayan Wira, Ni Madé Wiratini, and many, many others. There has not been room to credit individual informants for their contributions during the course of the text.

In addition, what I learned from these artists might never have grown inside of me had it not been for the musicians of Gamelan Sekar Jaya in the California Bay Area, with whom I shared year after year of high adventure. The same holds for members of Gamelan Sekar Kembar in New Haven, Connecticut, who demonstrated a quickness and enthusiasm that surprised even some jaded Balinese experts. Other teachers and friends of the music to whom expressions of gratitude are due include Frank Bennett, Martin Bresnick, Mantle Hood, Dieter Mack, David Mott, Danker Schaareman, Andrew Toth, Andreas Varsanyi and Bonnie Wade.

Finally, thanks also to my parents, my fantastic wife Pam, and, at last, Molly.

Michael Tenzer
Hamden, Connecticut

Putu Widiantini performs Kebyar Gandrung (a dance similar to Taruna Jaya), backed up by drummer Wayan Sudirana.

CHAPTER ONE

An Introduction to Balinese Music

"It is the opening day of the temple feast, and the children have assembled at the house to carry their gamelan to the temple. I give them each a cloth of large black and white check for a headdress, which will mark them as a club, and they all proceed to pick bright red blossoms from the hibiscus shrubs and put them in their hair. They then take their instruments and go out in dignified single file, while I follow behind. On the way to the temple someone suddenly remembers that the gamelan has never been blessed and purified. This is a bad start, but, on reaching the temple, we find that it can be done on the spot, for there are both priest and holy water, and we may have the benefit of offerings already prepared for other purposes. The arrival of the gamelan has caused much excited comment. The other club is already there, and the two gamelan are set in opposite pavilions. The ceremony of blessing the instruments is performed, and the children are told to play one piece as a termination of the rite. They sit down, and people eagerly crowd around, their curiosity aroused by the size of the children and the presence of the surprising angklung. The priest asks them to stand back. It is the children's hour; they dominate the scene. The women pause in their offerings and stand by; the adult club watches from the pavilion. The priest says 'Enggeh, tabuhin! (Well, strike up!)' and the children begin, while everyone listens in silence, smiling with pleasure. Suddenly for once,

the Balinese seem almost sentimental. There is no doubt that the children are a success."

—Composer-musicologist Colin McPhee, describing the debut of a children's music club that he sponsored in Sayan village, Bali, 1938.[1]

Music lovers have long discerned a splendid aural feast in the sounds of the *gamelan*. Emanating perpetually from communities all over the island of Bali, its sonorities sail over the ricefields on clear nights, showering the air with brilliant cascades of metallic sound, lonely whispering melodies, grandiose and clangorous marches, virtuosic rhythms, and breathtaking crescendos. Animated with the sounds of drums, flutes and gongs, it is a compelling experience that persists in the mind's ear long after its pulsations fade.

The ethereal music of the gamelan is sustained with an esthetic that prizes

Gamelan angklung performing at a temple ceremony in the village of Kedewatan.

---

1 From McPhee, Colin, *Children and Music in Bali*, taken from Belo, Jane, ed. *Traditional Balinese Culture*, Columbia University Press, New York 1970. The article was originally written in 1939 for the periodical *Djawa*; it was subsequently revised in 1954.

beautiful melody and a refined sense of formal design. This is not a music characterized by the sweeping emotions of romanticism; rather it is detailed, secure in construction, and full of insistent rhythms and elegant patterns. In the music's rich abstractions the listener encounters clarity and complexity that make it one of the most rewarding musical experiences to be had on our planet. These rewards are multiplied when one considers the music within the context of the remarkable place and culture that support it, the island of Bali.

Music is ubiquitous in Bali; its abundance is far out of proportion to the dimensions of the island. The Hindu-Balinese religion (officially known as Agama Hindu Dharma) requires gamelan for the successful completion of most of the tens of thousands of ceremonies undertaken yearly. At a plethora of traditionally mandated religious events, the gods descend in numbers to inhabit their designated shrines for the length of the festivities, awaiting the lavish musical entertainments that their village hosts are expected to provide. For the procession of offerings into the temple, there is music; for the spilling of cremated souls' ashes into the sea, there is music; for the exorcism of evil spirits, there is music; and for the ritual filing of teeth, there is music.

And for dance there is music. In Bali these two art forms are wedded in spirit, nuance, structure and even terminology. Balinese choreography, in its purest interpretation, is a detailed and subtle, physical embodiment of the music that accompanies it. Music and dance together are a mutually reflective duet—two realizations of the same abstract beauty, each clothed in the attributes of its form. For the gods, dance is as important a part of their visits to the earthly plane as is music. For the Balinese people these two arts are an inexorable combination, and to participate in the performance of either is a coveted privilege.

The Balinese embellish this rigorous schedule of sacred musical events with a wide range of more worldly occasions in which gamelan also assumes a crucial role. There are flirtatious street dances, frenzied bull races, and gamelan performances for guests and dignitaries. A regular cycle of gamelan competitions and festivals provides a forum for people to demonstrate their pride in their musical abilities and their dedication to the cultivation of a priceless cultural heritage for its own sake, independent of the ritual needs that it fills.

Gamelan Music: Sound, Language and Aesthetic

In a general way, the word "gamelan" (pronounced gah-meh-*lan*) means orchestra, or the music played by the orchestra, but it corresponds to the Western sense of that word only in that it conjures up an image of a group of people making music together. To be precise, gamelan refers to the instruments themselves, which exist as an inseparable set, and not to a group of individuals who gather to play upon them. The components of the gamelan come in many combinations, tunings, and sizes, each with specific religious or secular functions. There are almost as many different kinds of gamelan in Bali as there are occasions for them to be heard. The term gamelan itself derives from a Javanese verb meaning 'to handle'; the indigenous Balinese pronunciation has a 'b' at the beginning of the second syllable: *gambelan*. A general term for the art of playing music is *karawitan*. Gamelan compositions are referred to as *tabuh* (also an older word for the mallets used to play the instruments), *gending*, or *lagu*, which is really an Indonesian word for melody.

At the center of Balinese musical culture are the deep and penetrating reverberations of the bronze gongs. When the raised center, or boss, of a large gong is struck, a powerful bass tone emerges, the sound of which has inspired the reverence of Balinese for centuries. Gongs, as the strongest and most important timbre in most gamelan, legislate the character of the set of instruments to which they belong. A gamelan, so it is said, is only as good as its gong. Enjoying the support of the gong's anchoring are the drums, flutes and keyed metal instruments (metallophones) that comprise the remainder of the ensemble. Most of these instruments are constructed primarily of bronze, but some are made wholly from bamboo, and a few others from more esoteric materials. Each has its own name and definite musical function. Normally they all must play together in order for the music to sound as it should.

Sets of gamelan instruments are usually owned and maintained by village wards called *banjar*, which call upon their citizenry to fill the places in the ensemble. When the members of a gamelan group get together to make music, they do not improvise, except within strict limits. They play music that has been fully composed and planned out in advance of rehearsals, learned by rote, and painstakingly practiced, coordinated and polished until the desired musical standard has been achieved. There is little if any room for the individual to express him or herself in gamelan performance; instead the ideal is the cultivation of absolute coordination and channeling of each member's artistic personality into a unified musical expression. The very elements of the music are constructed so as to aid in this process, as we shall see throughout this book.

Just as the building-blocks of the music are illustrative of their larger context, so too are the terms and vocalizations with which the Balinese talk about gamelan and sing its tunes and rhythms. Amongst the hundreds of onomatopoetic words that pepper the indigenous Balinese language (thoroughly distinct from Bahasa Indonesia, the national language) and give it an inherent musicality of its own, there are many that refer to gamelan. The sounds of these words reveals much of importance about Balinese aesthetic concerns and the connections that are perceived between music and natural surroundings. For instance, *tekep* (which sounds almost like t-k'p because the consonants are so heavily accented in speech) is a clean and sharp-edged word that denotes the crucial technique of using the fingers to stop the resonance of the bronze keys and gongs in melodic passages. Any gamelan that has not mastered *matetekep* (mah-t'-t'-k'p), the art of tekeping, can expect to produce no more than a pathetically unfocussed blur of reverberating bronze.

The words *incep* (in-che') and *resik* (re-si'), used to describe the highest degrees of precision and togetherness that a full gamelan ensemble may strive to achieve, are pronounced with marked glottal stops and heavy stresses that mimic the crisp, economical unity that is so highly prized in performance. In contrast, *romon* (roh-mohn) and *rontog* (rohn-tohg), denoting music so sloppily played that it merits hisses and ridicule, are enunciated with lengthy second syllables that are difficult to utter cleanly. With apologies for dwelling on the negative for a moment, another colorful Balinese idiom typically hurled at underprepared musicians is *batu malablab* (bah-too m'lub-lub). *Batu* means rock or stone, and *malablab* is the active form of the incisively onomatopoetic verb "to boil." A gamelan deserving of the sobriquet "boiling rock" is likely going nowhere fast.

The Balinese solfége syllables (scale tone naming system, see Chapter Three) are mellifluously based around changing vowel sounds within one word: *ding*, *dong*, *deng*, *dung* and *dang*. When pronounced in succession an extraordinarily clear harmonic line is created, one perhaps more evoca-

Colin McPhee (1900–1964), composer and ethnographer of Balinese music.

tive of an actual scale than the Western do, re, and mi. The syllables *dug* and *dag*, used to emulate certain Balinese drum strokes, might give rise to a series like *dug du' dug d' da dug da dug* when voiced in rapid succession imitating true drum patterns. With its random distribution of accents, this kind of phrase has been compared to the amusing spectacle of a chicken jerkily pecking on the ground for grains of rice. Associated with the same image is *nyog cag* (nyog-chag),[2] a term for a special style of rapid-fire melodic ornamentation. If additional evidence of gamelan-like activity in the animal kingdom is required, anyone who has spent an evening in the Balinese countryside can attest to the polyphonic, rhythmic croaking of frogs in the ricefields as being perhaps the most plentiful source of inspiration for local musicians.

Reflections in the natural environment and the thorough integration of gamelan into the communally based lifestyle of the Balinese provide a certain appeal that goes beyond pure considerations of sonic and structural beauty. Musicians everywhere seek recognition and reward for their art, but Bali is one of a handful of places in the world where there seems to be, at least at face value, a much greater overall respect granted to the role of music in sustaining the very foundations of society. We need not romanticize, as many have done, in order to discover the reality behind this assertion. Balinese musical culture will seem all the more remarkable after a sober assessment. Besides, the image of Bali as an idyll is a misleading oversimplification, as is the perception of the Balinese artist as a primitive living in an unchanging and perfect state of balance and harmony. In light of this, the achievement of Balinese music can be seen as a particularly extraordinary one. Perhaps this helps to explain the fascination that it has long held for foreigners.

International Reputation: Colin McPhee

A much-celebrated encounter between French composer Claude Debussy and the music of a Javanese court gamelan took place when a group from Java performed at the Paris International Exhibition in 1889. Debussy's works had already demonstrated certain characteristics akin to those of Javanese music, and his enthusiasm for the music he heard has generated ongoing debate amongst musicians as to whether his subsequent compositions specifically reflect the influence of the gamelan.[3] A complex question to answer, perhaps, but nonetheless a starting point for observing the slowly accelerating filtering of gamelan music into the consciousness of Western musicians and audiences.

---

2 Ruby Ornstein provided the *nyog cag* anecdote in her dissertation *Gamelan Gong Kebyar: The Development of a Balinese Musical Tradition* (UCLA, 1971) p. 227.

3 For an in-depth discussion of this issue, see Mueller, Richard *Javanese Influence in Debussy's Fantaisie and Beyond* in the *Journal of Nineteenth Century Music*, Fall 1986.

The first Balinese group to tour abroad was the ensemble from Peliatan village, which played in Paris in 1931. A much more lavish and extensive tour by the same ensemble took place in 1952, organized by British entrepreneur John Coast. The group was a sensation in London, New York and Las Vegas and impressed the intricacies of Balinese music and dance on an international audience for the first time.

In the 1920s, the Odeon company released some recordings made in Bali. These came to the attention of Colin McPhee, a young Canadian-born composer living in New York. McPhee was an *enfant terrible* on the contemporary music stage of the time, possessed of the daring and idealism characteristic of the musical life of the era. He was immediately captivated by the recordings. The sounds of Balinese music awoke in him a singular ambition to hear the music at its source and to document it as fully as possible, setting aside (temporarily, he supposed) a promising career. He arrived on the island in 1931 and lived there more or less continuously until the forebodings of war necessitated his hasty departure some 8 years later.

McPhee arrived in Bali at a time of unbelievable musical activity. Village cultural life was aglow with creative freedom abetted by the ongoing decline of the courts and the shifting of artistic centers from the palaces to the banjar. He quickly mustered a retinue of friends, teachers and informants who helped him to realize his dream of a thorough record of the musical life of the era. A Steinway grand piano in the front room of his house in Sayan village was an object of delight for many Balinese, helping to make his home a favored meeting spot for well-known musicians. Working in tandem with Western colleagues such as anthropologist Margaret Mead and painter Walter Spies, McPhee became an expert on Balinese culture. His dedication and benevolence motivated him to act as a patron as well; he helped to reconstruct and revitalize many older styles of music in danger of extinction.

After his return home, McPhee never succeeded in recapturing the sense of inspiration and purpose that had been his while in Bali. During the subsequent period of his life he remained possessed by the charms of gamelan but found it difficult to communicate his enthusiasm to others, for whom the exotic remoteness of the island and its music remained a formidable barrier. McPhee's single acclaimed composition after 1930, Tabuh-Tabuhan, was a fantasia-like meditation for full Western orchestra based on Balinese musical ideas. Over the years the piece and a few other works of his have been performed by major symphony orchestras throughout North America and Europe. He composed but little in the following decades, and found himself mostly in personal and financial hard times until towards the end of his life, when he accepted a professorship at the University of California at Los Angeles. Here he devoted his remaining years to scholarly pursuits and the establishing of a gamelan study program at the school.

McPhee's life ended in both triumph and tragedy. He died in 1964, only a few weeks after finishing his magnum opus, *Music in Bali* (Yale Univ. Press, New Haven, 1966), for decades the most exhaustive volume available on the subject in any language. He had been at work on it for over thirty years but did not live to see the final page proofs. The book is a masterpiece of detail and organization that was quickly recognized as a classic in the fields of ethnography and music. Others have since researched Balinese gamelan—including many notable Balinese scholars—but all acknowledge a great debt to McPhee's thorough scholarship. The present book's modest ambitions would have been unrealizable without it.

Had he lived a few more years, Colin McPhee would have enjoyed more of the fruits of his labor. Appreciation of Balinese music has burgeoned internationally and its echoes can be heard resonating in the creations of contemporary composers throughout the world. In the footsteps of the Peliatan gamelan—with whom McPhee was closely associated—Balinese groups perform abroad constantly. His study group at UCLA became a model for similar groups worldwide. And as for McPhee's most ardent concern for the continued vitality of traditional Balinese music, he would have been gratified to learn that many of the rare styles for whose continued existence he feared have been preserved, in many cases as a direct consequence of his initial efforts.

CHAPTER TWO

A Brief History of the
Music Through the
Late Twentieth Century

Early in the first millennium A.D., a bronze-age technology emerged in Southeast Asia that ultimately facilitated the manufacture of musical instruments. The musicians of the Philippine *kulintang,* the *pi phat* of Thailand, and related ensembles in Burma, Cambodia and other places in that part of the continent all use bronze gongs in making music to this day. But it is in Java and neighboring Bali that the most development occurred, and it is exclusively these two places with which the term "*gamelan*" is associated.[1] In Java there are many independent traditions; best known among them are the exalted and complex musics of the Central Javanese courts Surakarta and Yogyakarta, and the more robust village gamelan of West Java (Sunda). These are but two of the many regions that sustain a rich repertoire there. Music in Java is a subject that has filled many volumes, but it is wholly outside the domain of the present book.

Balinese music ultimately traces important parts of its origins to Java, and even now the two islands' musics share similar instruments, tuning systems and general principles of organization. But beyond that, the music they each produce reflects the vast differences between their cultures and

---

1 Gamelan was introduced in Malaysia during the 19th century, and is still cultivated there in a few places.

the temperaments of their peoples. Both are highly sophisticated, but while the courtly Javanese music is reflective, subdued, and wide open to the contributions of individual performers' lovingly crafted improvisations, Balinese music—especially that of the 20th century—is a juggernaut of brash and aggressive energy, deriving much of its effect from virtuoso ensemble coordination and dramatic contrasts in mood. While there is improvisation in Balinese music, it is subordinate to unity and precision.

Bali and Java also share a history of monarchism and have benefited from the influence of the courts as patrons of the arts. Both maintain a strong attachment to the mythology of Hindu culture, which is especially remarkable in Java given the completion of its transition to Islam over 500 years ago. In Bali the limited geographic area and the native animism with which Hinduism combined served to insure the firm implantation of the gamelan tradition outside the palace walls as well, imbuing it with more of the visceral characteristics of a village music and allowing it to proliferate as a popular art even after the kingdoms crumbled and Indonesia asserted herself as a nation.

Balinese music is first and foremost an oral tradition. While a kind of musical notation does exist, players almost never use it. All music is passed down from generation to generation through the guru-disciple relationship. Musical style develops through the years in relation to changing public tastes and private patronages, the inspiration of creative musicians, and the general development of Balinese society.

The further back one reaches in time, the more difficult it is to be specific about the history of Balinese music. Scant information in the form of bas-reliefs (mostly at Borobudur and other sites in Java) offer some clues as to what music may have been like during the latter part of the first millennium A.D., when Hinduism swept through what is now the Indonesian archipelago. The temple carvings depict instruments in use at the time. Scattered *lontar* (palm leaf manuscripts) from later eras offer more about the cosmological significance of musical activity than they do about the content and practice of the music itself.

The tale of a musical culture's development is always closely connected to its social history as well as to the availability of technology and materials for building musical instruments. The many distinctive colors and styles of indigenous Balinese singing—some open relaxed and full, others tight, ornamented, and constrained—each emerged from a particular historical period, and continue to evoke it when heard today. Some ancient songs are for robust choruses of villagers intended to encourage trance states during rituals, others are the esoteric *sotto voce* intonations of priests, still others are loud and penetrating, sung solo by actors in theatrical performance.

While bamboo, hardwoods and cowhide were always at hand for fashioning flutes, drums and simple keyed percussion instruments, it was the arrival of bronze culture from mainland Asia sometime prior to Hinduism that made the decisive difference for Javanese and Balinese music. As smiths learned to perfect techniques for casting gongs and later, forging slabs (keys), systems of tuning evolved, as did ways of combining the resulting instruments into ensembles.

One of the earliest Balinese ensembles for which written descriptions exist is the *gamelan gambuh.* It is mentioned in early lontar as the accompaniment to the *gambuh* play, which portrays episodes in the life of the legendary Hindu-Javanese prince Panji, drawn mainly from the old Javanese epic poem Malat. Still extant in Batuan village, Gianyar District, Pedungan near Denpasar, Depehe east of Singaraja, and a few other villages, this ensemble gives some sense of what Balinese gamelan may have been like about five to seven hundred years ago. The instruments represent what was probably state-of-the-art craftsmanship at the time.

Four deep-voiced bamboo *suling* (flutes) are the core of the gamelan. They are so long that, sitting cross-legged, a player must place the end of the suling on the ground some distance in front of him to be able to reach the mouthpiece properly. These suling, accompanied by the *rebab* bowed spike fiddle spin airy, haunting melodies in a kind of fuzzy coordination that have a distinctive, ghostly sound.

The tuned metallophones so prominent in later Balinese gamelan were not yet being produced at that time. Instead, the percussion section of the ensemble is led by two high-pitched drums and filled out by a pair of small bronze gongs and a battery of indefinitely pitched bells, cymbals and chimes that underpin the melodies with a carpet of bright ringing accents. Altogether the effect is that of a music hovering in space restlessly; heard today it vividly evokes the bygone era that fostered it. An excerpt of the gambuh composition Tabuh Gari—a well-known melody used as a kind of overture to the performance—is heard on the book CD, track 4.

Gambuh ensemble from North Bali, circa 1857.

While certain sacred ensembles still heard in Bali today may in fact be older, the musical architecture of gambuh melodies is a crucial precursor to nearly all Balinese music of the last several centuries. The musical principles and practices evident in gamelan gambuh compositions are still very much a part of modern Balinese music. The utilization of a firmly grounded core melody (here, the suling and rebab), propelled onward and controlled for speed and dynamics by a pair of drums, and punctuated cyclically by gongs, comprise the backbone of most Balinese gamelan. That these techniques are so well-established in gambuh shows that they are quite ancient. The employment of gongs to delineate so-called circular, repeating melodic cycles, particularly salient and pervasive in gamelan, stands in contrast to Western classical music, which generally proceeds from beginning to end in a comparatively straight line. But these are imperfect visual analogies that cannot do justice to the many sensations of time's passage that music evokes. Some have suggested that the periodic and regenerative structures of gamelan melodies make an apt metaphor for the life, death, and reincarnation cycles so central to Balinese Hindu belief. Whether or not this connection can be academically substantiated, the analogy provides an apt description.

Music in the Courts

The spread of Islam throughout the archipelago during the 13th to 15th centuries steadily undermined the powerful Hindu Majapahit empire of East Java, leading to its gradual collapse in the 1400s. Beginning in the late 1300s conditions compelled the royal entourages to take refuge on the Hindu stronghold of Bali. Their culture subsequently blended in with the existing Hindu/animistic beliefs of the native Balinese. The concurrent subjugation of local rulers, along with the formation of new kingdoms and a new social hierarchy, laid the foundation for a flowering of all Balinese arts. From that time until the arrival of the Dutch colonialists some four hundred years later, Balinese music blossomed largely in splendid isolation, producing a variety of forms, ensembles, and styles remarkable in their diversity.

The descendants of the Majapahit rulers, firmly ensconced in their royal palaces in what are now the capital district (Denpasar) and eight *kabupaten* (regions) of Bali, were great patrons of music on the whole, and more often than not avid practitioners themselves. Gambuh was cultivated in the courts, as was the singing of lontar texts known as *kidung* and *kakawin*. With the advancement of bronze technology and the appearance of finely crafted gongs (to this day, though, the best of the large gongs are cast exclusively in Java) and metal keys, the bronze-based gamelan became prevalent in the courts and temples.

Musical accompaniment was *de rigueur* for an array of secular and sacred occasions of ritual, theater, and even just plain recreation. The famous sweetly-tuned *gamelan semar pegulingan* (from *Semar,* the god of love and *pegulingan,* pillows room) played outside the king's bedchamber during afternoons of royal passion, using melodies ingeniously adapted from the gambuh repertoire for the full complement of bronze instruments. The enormous *gong gdé* (great gong) orchestra, found today only in a few villages, accompanied ritual male dancers and provided music for state and religious occasions—with a group of majestic instrumental compositions that to this day are heard in all temples at festival time. These dignified slow pieces, known as *lelambatan,* were nurtured during the post-Majapahit era and in many ways can be thought of as the soul of Balinese orchestral music.

The independent kingdoms, the talents and musical interests of their individual rulers, and their topographically necessitated isolation from one another, largely account for the great variation in musical styles that is in evi-

I Ketut Maria (sec Chapter Six) dances the Kebyar Duduk during the nascent years of *kebyar* style.

dence today. For example, the *legong* dance and its music, which by most accounts originated in the south-central courts of Sukawati and Blahbatuh during the late 19th century, quickly became popular throughout the surrounding areas, but made few inroads into the northern and western parts of the island. Those areas, however, maintained and continue to maintain special gamelan whose origins in these places contribute to each one's distinctive cultural personality.

The Colonial Period

The Dutch encroachment into Bali was gradual during the 19th century and limited to the northern coastal regions. Eventually they stormed southern Bali, resulting in the infamous *puputan* (mass ritual suicides) of the members of the Badung (1906) and Semarapura (formerly Klungkung; 1908) courts on the battlefield. These dramatic events helped to solidify Dutch control of the entire island, and soon a colonial administration was firmly in place. Though the Dutch were savvy enough to foster good relations with the kings when practicable, in effect the decline of the courts and their artistic patronages was at hand. Major cultural and social upheavals resulted when the musical traditions (and instruments) that had previously been largely the domain of the higher castes were now passed down to the villagers.

The most significant musical event from the early part of the Dutch period was the birth of the *gamelan gong kebyar* in the villages of North Bali around 1915. This gamelan, a radical modernization of the standard temple orchestra, swept Bali in the following decades. *Kebyar* style became the *lingua franca* of Balinese music as no other type of orchestral repertoire had before. The high speed and virtuoso pyrotechnics of kebyar music are quintessentially 20th century in flavor, and bear the unmistakable stamp of a music at long last released from the precious refinery of aristocratic environs.

Up until kebyar completed this swift ascent, the *gamelan pelegongan* had reigned supreme in the southern part of Bali. This orchestra, derived from the semar pegulingan but intended primarily for accompanying legong dances, was at the time a fertile area for musical creation and experimentation. The great composer and teacher I Wayan Lotring of Kuta village, whose shadow towered over the island's musical world during this period, composed brilliant pieces and taught many village groups the subtleties of the style. His name is still mentioned today with reverence.

But soon villages were transforming their gamelan pelegongan into kebyar as fast as they could melt down the delicate bronze keys and recast them for the heavier, larger instruments of the new gamelan. The best-known teacher of kebyar from this period was Gdé Manik of Jagaraga village in kabupaten Buleleng. He zealously taught the dynamic new music—which he had helped to create—to villages all over the south, where it was embraced enthusiastically.

Once Lotring and other musicians got their hands on kebyar, however, they enhanced the vocabulary of the music by imbuing it with some of the particular subtleties of pelegongan and other court-influenced styles rooted in South Bali. It is in fact the flexibility of kebyar and its ability to evoke the music of other gamelan to a certain convincing degree that has accounted for its staying power. Even now in the north, though, some purist groups continue to promulgate as much as they have been able to retain of the undiluted original, full of its own refinements and surprises, to which they proudly lay claim.

Colin McPhee's presence in Bali during the 1930s resulted in his documentation of the awesome proliferation of musical activity in the villages during the colonial period. In addition to the types discussed herein, he covered many other styles that flourished—some sacred, some secular, some popular, some on the decline. With their new roles as successors to the custody of gamelan traditions, the village gamelan clubs and the teachers that led them brought about a great flowering of musical culture, effervescent with change and creativity.

Music from Indonesian Independence to the Orde Baru

The years 1940–1965 were a time of war, liberation, revolution, political turmoil and even natural disaster in Bali. Gunung Agung erupted in 1962 just prior to an important ceremony at Besakih temple. The task of nation-building dominated the local scene much as it did throughout the new Republic of Indonesia. Inevitable responsibilities and conflicts made it difficult for Balinese to devote their energies to the arts as they had under the relative stability of colonial rule. But musical activity, albeit somewhat curtailed, did continue apace.

Gamelan gong kebyar, by now deeply entrenched in even the most remote villages, was so familiar that it was enough to simply use the word "gong" to refer to it. President Sukarno, himself part Balinese, was very fond of kebyar and often invited groups to perform at his behest in either Jakarta or at his Bali hideaway in Tampaksiring. At his suggestion a flurry of realist, nationalistically-oriented music and dance pieces were created during the early 1960s, but as this was at the opposite esthetic pole from the abstract, fantastical nature of most Balinese art, they did not find favor for long. 1965 brought turmoil to Bali and Indonesia, as the process of purging suspected communists led to the massacre of hundreds of thousands and the eventual ouster of Sukarno. His successor, Suharto, led the country under the banner of the quasi-totalitarian *Orde Baru* (New Order) until 1998.

The obsession with kebyar was producing musicians of great technical skill. Their exuberance buoyed the music to ever increasing levels of speed and complexity. But at the same time, so much of the musical heritage—and the refined temperament embodied in the older styles—was suffering from neglect. This lamentable state of affairs was addressed in the early 1960s with the establishment of a High School and a College of the Arts in Denpasar. The high school is known as KOKAR/SMKI and the college-conservatory as ISI (formerly STSI, and before that ASTI; the name changes reflect successive upgrades in the school's institutional and degree-conferring status). ISI (www.isi-dps.ac.id), meaning *Institut Seni Indonesia*—Indonesian Institute of the Arts—offers study in music, dance, shadow play arts, and several kinds of visual arts and design. These schools are part of a nationwide system that includes campuses around the archipelago. The faculty, drawn from the ranks of the best artists, are entrusted with the tasks of teaching, academic research, the active preservation of older styles, and the creation of new works.

The notion of imposing academic legitimacy on a music which had always thrived in its natural environment was at first viewed askance. After all, reasoned parents, why should I send my child to a school in Denpasar when there's plenty of music right here in our village? Soon, as the reputation of the faculties grew and Indonesia moved toward adopting the standards of a global community which stresses the benefits of obtaining a degree, resistance lessened. Nowadays it is simply assumed that a serious young musician should get a formal education if he or she plans to earn an income from music. By the late 1970s the schools had become an influential cultural powerhouse calling the shots for innovations in musical style. New works by the schools' composers and choreographers emanated prolifically from the campuses and were adopted instantly almost everywhere. This wave of change eventually partially self-corrected as new attention to the importance of preserving regional styles took hold. But sometimes it was too little, too late. Today KOKAR and ISI, because of the way in which they dominate the scene more than any individual village or court ever did, remain controversial.

Another important factor in the modern history of Balinese music is the advent of mass tourism. Many complain that musical standards tend to relax when a group performs for 'undiscerning' foreigners, but this notion is open to question and difficult to generalize about. Tourism is a kind of new patronage, and a great incentive for gamelan in tourist areas—both financially and in terms of civic pride. The Ubud/Peliatan district, for example, as anxious to preserve its reputation as a center for the arts as it is to sell tickets for nightly tourist shows, now boasts dozens of active ensembles. With the economic prosperity such villages enjoy, more gamelan are bought and more groups formed than ever before.

Even in villages off the beaten track, the late twentieth century saw a renaissance of musical activity. Yearly government-sponsored island-wide gamelan competitions and the Bali Arts Festival, held every June and July in Denpasar, provide high profile performance opportunities for groups all over Bali. Cassette companies flourished in the 1970s–90s, competing for a growing market of consumers seeking good recordings of classical and modern gamelan music. Television and radio stations broadcast performances daily. A general sense of the importance of seeing traditional Balinese music through the tumultuous developments of the era was deeply felt by most. Most importantly, Balinese music is as essential for ceremonial and religious purposes as ever, and that state of affairs shows few signs of changing.

In the academies, and to some extent in the villages, the kebyar craze has peaked. In the early 2000s it partly ceded ground to the diverse musical developments discussed in Chapter Ten, which are better appreciated with reference to the fuller story of the music presented in the intervening pages. Young composers are turning more and more to older types of gamelan for inspiration, while at the same time inventing musical techniques that stretch the boundaries of what is traditionally "correct." Only a musical culture very secure with itself could tolerate such experimentation. Moreover, interaction and collaboration with musicians from all over the world have become commonplace. This kind of cross-cultural fertilization is a natural development here, where valuable new ideas have always been accepted and cleverly transformed to meet the needs of the Balinese. It seems likely that the future of Balinese music is bright, even as gamelan musicians confront the array of new problems and influences resulting from Bali's drastically expanded national and international profiles.

Kempur and *klentong*, *gamelan semar pegulingan*, Ketewel village.

CHAPTER THREE

The Construction and Tuning of Instruments

Kerajinan Gong Siddha Karya (Siddha Karya Gong Enterprise), located just northeast of Blahbatuh village off the main road to Gianyar, is one of only a few gamelan foundries in Bali. Pandé Wayan Pager, and before him his father Pandé Madé Gableran, who in turn was preceded by generations of forebears, have made the enterprise a family affair. There is another foundry steps away run by Gableran's brother Sukarta, plus a group of smiths (tracing to the same family line) in the village of Tihingan, near Semarapura; one in Binong, northwest of Denpasar, and one more in North Bali at Sawan, southeast of Singaraja. The honorific *pandé* always precedes a gamelan maker's name because metalsmiths belong to the pandé clan, an exclusive lineage that has had the sacred responsibility of casting musical instruments and other important metal objects (such as krisses) for centuries. Balinese musicians trust Siddha Karya's workers with the manufacture of new sets of instruments and the maintenance and repair of old ones. The business acts as a broker for the import and sale of large Javanese gongs and also for non-bronze instruments (such as drums) which are made in Bali but assembled elsewhere. Pandé Pager is heir to a rarefied art, a skillful technician, and a smart, prosperous entrepreneur.

Gamelan instruments at all stages of production are in evidence during a walk through the interconnected courtyards of the family compound. On the

Instrument case carvers in Singapadu village.

right, just beyond the entrance is the foundry proper. Scraps of *kerawang*, a bronze consisting of approximately three parts copper to ten parts tin, sit in small piles on pieces of banana trunk waiting to be weighed. The alloy is mixed here from raw materials, although it is considered better to reuse old kerawang when possible, such as may be obtained from instruments or other bronze objects broken beyond repair. Between one and two kilograms of metal is used per key or small gong, depending on the size of the instrument for which it is intended. Once the furnace at the rear is hot, the kerawang is melted at a searing temperature and fired for some time to insure a good blend. When it is removed, poured and allowed to solidify a bit, a gold vermillion form glows from within the mold. This is picked up gingerly with tongs, forged into the proper shape with a hammer, and plunged into a basin of water. After it is cool enough to handle it is filed, scraped and polished until the lustrous surface of a finished key is recognizable.

In the back of the workshop, carpenters are splayed out amidst saws, chisels, lumber and shavings. The *pelawah* (instrument cases) are constructed here. *Ketewel* or *nangka* (wood of the jack fruit tree), a heavy and durable semi-hardwood, is the preferred material, although other woods are sometimes used. Once the basic form of the pelawah is cut and assembled the carvers go to work, creating elaborate designs on every square centimeter of the wood's surface. Most patterns are standardized, featuring a pair of *bhoma* (earth spirits) or *naga* (mythical serpents) watching vigilantly from each end with the edges and corners filled in with flowers and other elaborate patterns. These are completed quickly and somewhat nonchalantly by craftsmen who have the designs at the tips of their fingers. Imaginative and wealthy customers may request something a bit more complex, such as different scenes from the Ramayana or Mahabharata epics portrayed on each of a group of instruments, and as a result some gamelan are unique works of art. Once the carving is completed the wood is varnished or decorated with paint and gold leaf.

At the central pavilion the instruments are tuned and assembled. This requires expertise and a sensitive ear, and is entrusted only to a pandé. If the instrument involved is a set of keys to be part of a *gamelan gong kebyar*, for example, and if no specific tuning is requested by the customer, the scale will be copied from a "family standard" set of keys that the tuner keeps beside him for reference.

The pitch of a key can be lowered by shaving some bronze from the underside, as this makes the key longer in proportion to its diminishing thickness and causes it to vibrate more slowly when struck. Filing along one of the ends shortens the key; consequently it vibrates more quickly and is higher in pitch. When the whole set is in tune, the keys are strung up in ascending order by looping twin strips of rawhide (or some sort of cord) through two holes that have been drilled, one at both ends of each key. The cord is secured with wooden pegs under each hole, and the whole set of keys is suspended over the pelawah by tautly tying the ends of the cords through eye hooks placed at either side of the wooden frame. The length of the cord is supported at intervals by little posts that act as trestles to keep each key freely suspended over its own bamboo resonator.

These bamboo tubes, snugly nestled into holes in the pelawah, must also be tuned so that the column of air that they support vibrates at the same rate as the key that hangs above it. The higher the pitch of the key, the shorter the resonating space needed. Bamboo, grows in sections separated by nodes; the tubes are cut so that the space above the node leaves the proper length of air for its key. The section of bamboo below the node is non-functional. When viewed from the front, the nodes can be seen ascending from left to right like a staircase.

Balinese Tuning Systems

The standard that each pandé uses for tuning a *gong kebyar* (or any other type of gamelan) is unique to their family. Other pandé have their own methods, as do many other craftsmen in Bali whose specialty is just to tune instruments, as distinct from casting the actual bronze. While there are common or popular tunings, there is no agreed upon norm that would make all gamelan on the island compatible with each other. This ensures that each set of instruments has its own characteristic sound and tonal personality. How different this is from the way things work in Western music, where the frequency of the note A above middle C is universally agreed upon at 440 vibrations per second (or very close to it)! With all other tones adjusted in relation to A440, it is possible for musicians anywhere to play together with ease. Such a situation is neither possible nor desirable in Bali. What is more, since most Balinese instruments are percussive, it is difficult to adjust their tuning to each other without going through the elaborate proce-dure described above. But despite the role of individual taste in determining the sound of a set of gamelan instruments, there is yet a theory of tuning and scales in Bali.

Rather than think of Balinese tunings as scales, it is perhaps helpful to conceive of them as a set of guidelines for intervals (distance relationships between tones). This idea is flexibly interpreted by tuners, giving rise to the variety of tunings found in actual practice. Two sets of guidelines, or systems for tuning, exist. Both in Bali and Java they are commonly known by the names *pélog* and *slendro*.

Pélog is a seven-note system in which notes are separated from each other by a series of unequal intervals. This is not as vague as it may sound, for there are generally accepted limitations as to how much the size of the intervals may either resemble one another or vary. A crude "sample" pélog collection can be obtained on the piano by starting at E and progressing upward on the white keys to the next D. However, this yields only half- and whole-step interval sizes, and no Balinese pélog is quite as uniform as that.

This scale and its many nuanced varieties is found in most older Balinese gamelan, such as *gambang*, *gambuh*, *semar pegulingan* and others. How-ever the full gamut of seven tones is rarely used during a single composi-tion. Instead, groups of five are isolated to form modes, each of which are named. A given piece usually restricts itself to the five tones of its mode. In gambuh and gamelan semar pegulingan repertoire each of the five tones used are labeled with one of the Balinese solfége names (similar to our *do, re, mi,* etc.) *ding, dong, deng, dung,* and *dang,* with *ding* considered to be the starting note of the mode. The chart below shows how the three modes *selisir, tembung* and *sunaren* are derived from the parent 7-tone pélog.[1]

parent pélog tones:	1	2	3	4	5	6	7
selisir mode:	ding	dong	deng	(—)	dung	dang	(—)
tembung mode:	dung	dang	(—)	ding	dong	deng	(—)
sunaren mode:	(—)	dung	dang	(—)	ding	dong	deng

But gambuh and semar pegulingan are rare and old ensembles. Most pélog-tuned gamelan in Bali are said to restrict themselves to tembung or selisir mode, both of which are distinguished by gaps after the tones *deng* and *dang*. (Sunaren is as well, but it is never mentioned as a source for tunings.) This combination of very wide intervals with comparatively narrow ones is responsible for the distinctive tonal character of most gamelan. No matter where the beginning of the mode lies in actual pitch—some gamelan may be higher, some lower—it is this succession of intervals which is its most identifiable feature. A possible selisir tuning on the piano could be played E-F-G-B-C; tembung could be played A-B-C-E-F.

The slendro system is inherently five tone.[2] It is found in the *gamelan gender wayang* used to accompany the shadow play, the *gamelan angklung*, and a few other ensembles. It also employs the *ding-dong-deng-dung-dang* syllabification of the tones. In contrast to the jagged, plaintive sound of the intervals in the 5-tone derivations of pélog, slendro is considered to be based on roughly equal intervals. Although in practice the distances between the tones are far from equivalent, slendro is nonetheless characterized by a smooth and harmonious progression. A very rough approximation of slendro could be played A-C-D-E-G, or on the black notes of the piano.

---

1 Other modes were formerly in use, associated with fingerings for flutes in gamelan gambuh. In addition, the sacred seven-tone ensembles gambang, selunding and luang make use of other mode classifications, which often vary from village to village. Today many of these are revived in the *gamelan semaradana* (see Chapter Ten).

2 Some contend that it is another subset of *pélog*, but this is an unusual point of view and difficult to substantiate.

With a little experience, novice listeners can learn to distinguish easily between the sounds of pélog and slendro, and also to appreciate the
subtle differences between gamelan tuned in like systems. But there is an
additional element in the tuning of any gamelan that is considered crucial,
above and beyond the system or mode employed. It is the factor that gives
gamelan music the pulsating, shimmering sound that travels so effortlessly
through the evening air; the key to making the instruments 'come alive'.

In Western music, when pairs of like instruments, say clarinets, play a
melody together on the same notes, we say that they are in unison. This
means that they are producing sound waves of exactly the same dimensions, making for the simplest and purest concordance of sounds. The next
purest would be at the interval of the octave, where one of the clarinets'
sound waves moves exactly twice as fast as the other's. This 2:1 ratio is
a kind of identity. We call a note that vibrates 880 times per second 'A'
just like the one an octave below it, which moves at half that speed, or
440 vibrations per second. Sound waves traveling together in such simple
mathematical relationships are perfectly synchronized and seem to our ears
to be smooth and stable. In Balinese music, such tones would be considered
wan and lifeless. Instead, pairs of instruments are intentionally tuned just
slightly apart from one another so that when the same tone is struck on the
two instruments simultaneously, the sound waves that emerge are of slightly different speeds. This causes an acoustical phenomenon called beating,
which makes the tones seem agitated and charged with pulsations.

Most gamelan vibrate, or beat, at a rate of somewhere between 5 and 8
times per second, depending on the preference of the gamelan's tuner and
the type of gamelan involved. In older styles of music the beating tends to
be slower, but in modern ones the extra intensity of rapid oscillations is
sought. In the case of a 7 vibration difference, every pair of instruments
from the lowest to the highest must be tuned so that the one vibrates 7
fewer times per second than the other. This is no mean feat, because while
that difference can account for a big discrepancy in pitch on the deep bass
instruments, it may be barely discernible in the piercing upper registers.
This is where the acute sensitivity of the tuner's ear really comes into play.
Furthermore, in order to keep the rate of beating constant throughout the
gamelan, octaves and other intervals within the scale must sometimes be
compromised. But the result is fantastic—a glorious bouquet of tones each

with its own character and relation to the whole. And when the full gamelan strikes up and a glistening cascade of sound rushes forth, the complexities of the tuning add a great deal to the intense visceral effect of the music.

Balinese Musical Instruments

The bronze instruments of the gamelan can be divided into two main groups: those with keys and those consisting of a gong or a group of gongs. Other types of instruments include barrel-shaped drums, bamboo flutes, cymbals, the bowed *rebab*, and a variety of other inventive music-making devices.

The keyed bronze metallophones in Balinese gamelan come in a number of different sizes and shapes and are struck with an assortment of different kinds of *panggul* (mallets). There are two basic structural designs for these instruments. Those in the *gender* (pronounced g'n-*dare*) family use bamboo resonators, above which the keys freely hang. In the *saron* (also called *gangsa jongkok*) family the keys are simply laid over a wooden trough, held in place with posts, and padded slightly with rubber where the bronze comes into contact with the wood. The sound is therefore more crisp and brittle than the sound of a gender. Sarons are fairly uncommon in Bali, but they are found in a few ensembles. In Java their presence is standard.

A gender is classified and given a specific name according to several criteria, including the register of its keys, the panggul with which it is played, and the ensemble in which it is used. The deepest-toned instruments, usually with 5 keys, are called *jegogan*; they are played with a single padded mallet and emit long ringing tones. An octave higher in range and also 5-keyed are the *calung,* sometimes called *jublag.* Another octave higher are the *penyacah,* but these are not always present. The function of this group of instruments is to play the core tones that form the basis for gamelan melody. They tend to play at a slower rate than the rest of the ensemble; in their sustained resonance the shimmering tuning of the orchestra is particularly audible.

The other group of gender in the gamelan are collectively known as *gangsa.* All are played with a hard wooden mallet and have from 7 to 12 keys, depending on the ensemble. These too come in three ranges. The largest and deepest, known as the *ugal* (or *giying*), is usually placed in the center. The ugal player sits on a high stool and leads the entire gangsa section. In the next octave are the 4 *pemadé*, and above them, at the peak of the

The Gamelan Gong Kebyar

Kantilan

Ugal

Pemadé

Pemadé

Kendang

Cengceng

Cengceng Kopyak

Jegogan

Calung

Calung

Pemadé

Pemadé

Rebab

Suling

Kendang

Gong

Kempur

Klentong

Reyong

Trompong

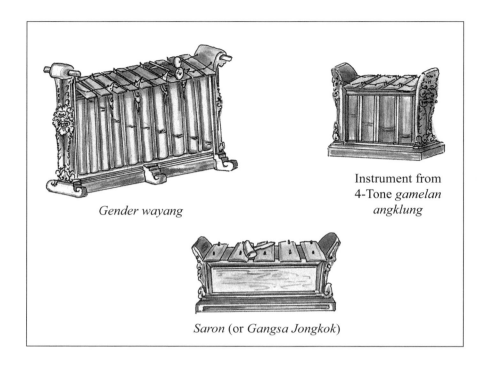

Gender wayang

Instrument from
4-Tone *gamelan
angklung*

Saron (or *Gangsa Jongkok*)

gamelan's range, are the 4 *kantilan*. The function of the pemadé and kantilan is to flesh out the core melody tones sounded by the bass instruments with developed melodies and elaborate ornamentations.

The term "gender" proper is reserved for instruments that are played with two rounded wooden mallets, one in each hand. They are found in certain gamelan where the delicate tonal color they produce is required. Lastly, the miniature 4-key gender-type metallophones of the gamelan angklung should be mentioned. Their melancholy tones can be heard at just about every temple in Bali whenever there is a ceremony.

The kinds of sounds that gender-type instruments are capable of producing are closely linked to the technique needed to play them. The lengthy resonances of the tones dictate that in any sequence of notes each tone must be stopped, or damped, either at the moment of or sometime before the arrival of the next one, in order to prevent the sounds from bleeding onto each other. For instruments played with a single mallet this is accomplished by grasping the key to be damped between the thumb and forefinger of the left hand. With two-mallet genders the fingertips and wrists are used. For slow passages these techniques merely require a little practice, but when the music gets fast—and does it get fast!—striking and damping motions follow each other in a wild blur of activity. But with the proper coordination and control the genders manage to emit a great range of sounds—from ear-splitting to nearly inaudible, and from silken smooth to biting staccato.

Gongs

The majestic gongs of Indonesia, and the technology for making them, form a central part of the archipelago's spiritual and cultural heritage. Particularly beautiful ones are prized as heirlooms, and are often thought to be the locus for strong magical and supernatural powers. In gamelan the gongs preside over the music like royalty at court, or like the heart over the mind and spirit.

Gongs used in Bali range in size from tiny high-pitched ones to enormous ones of 90 centimeters in diameter or more. With minor exceptions all are struck on the raised boss that protrudes from the middle of the gong's front surface; as with genders the deeper-toned ones require padded mallets. The smaller ones are hit with sticks wound with string for cushioning. Gongs aren't used or tuned in pairs the way keyed instruments are; the sound usually pulsates enough on its own to blend in well with the beating of the metallophones.

The most important function of the gongs in gamelan music is to mark structural points in a composition. The number of gongs employed for this purpose depends on the ensemble. Gong kebyar uses one or two *gong ageng* (the largest and deepest) for the beginnings and endings of melodies and other strong accents. If two, they are used in alternation and never together. Other divisions are the responsibility of the medium-sized *kempur*, the small, chiming *klentong* (or *kemong*), and the nearly ever-present *kempli*, whose clear, dry sound taps out the steady beat on which all musicians depend when the rhythms get tricky. Other types of gamelan make use of some of these gongs, plus others like the tiny *kelenang*, the flatbossed *kajar* and *bebende*, or a resonant version of the kempli called *tawa-tawa*.

Sets of 8 to 14 small gongs, arranged in ascending order of pitch and balanced on taut cords strung along a long wooden frame, are used in a melodic role. When such a set is played by a soloist it is called a *trompong*; when played by four people (each commandeering only a few of the gongs) it is called *reyong*. The former is known for its sophisticated melodic style and is usually associated with older ceremonial music. The reyong, mainly a 20th century development, is known for its dizzying ornamentations and 8-note brassy chords, formed by having each of the four players strike a gong with each hand. An older version of the reyong, in the *gamelan gong gdé*, requires only four gongs and two players.

No survey of bronze instruments would be complete without mention of the ubiquitous cymbals called *cengceng*. The enormous *cengceng kopyak* come in pairs and are similar to Western crash cymbals in manner of sound production. They are played in groups of at least four pairs, most often in ceremonial and processional gamelan. Most cengceng, though, are smaller and come in sets of six or more. All but two are set on a wooden base and struck by the unmounted ones, which are held by the player. The rapid-fire rhythms that result are an essential component of most any gamelan performance.

Drums and Other Instruments

Most gamelan are directed by a pair of *kendang* (drums). These are usually made of nangka wood shaped into a tapering cylinder and hollowed out in the middle in an hourglass shape. Skins are affixed at both ends by means of a long rawhide strip laced back and forth between the heads in an N-pattern, and tightened with sliding rings to control the tension on the heads. Kendang vary in size; the smaller the drum the more delicate the style of music with which it is associated.

Kendang are held across the lap and played on both heads with the fingers and hands, although sometimes a panggul is used in the right hand. In each pair the higher-pitched one is designated the *lanang* (male), and the lower-pitched the *wadon* (female).[3] The drums produce a variety of sounds (each named with the usual flair for onomatopoetic syllables)—like *kap, pak, dag, tut,* and so on—and an intricate technique for playing them has evolved. The sounds of the resonant *dag* and *tut*, made on the right skin, merge with gongs to generate a current of low register rhythm, while the crackling, unpitched *kap* and *pak* slice like a knife through the texture.

---

3 This curious reversal of male and female (human) voice characteristics applies also to pairs of gongs and other similar couplings. Female is deeper in pitch because it is associated with the earth, creation, and fertility.

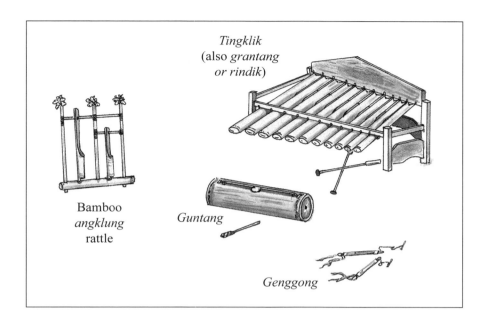

Tingklik
(also *grantang*
or *rindik*)

Bamboo
angklung
rattle

Guntang

Genggong

While one's attention is at first naturally drawn to the gamelan melodies they support, the rhythms of the Balinese kendang are in fact the motor that drives the orchestra.

Many instruments popular in Bali are made solely of bamboo tubes strung up in wooden frames. Such instruments are light, inexpensive, relatively easy to make, and are usually associated with recreational rather than ritual music. The most often encountered ones are known variously as *tingklik*, *grantang* or *rindik*. They are the sort of instruments that people keep around the house to fool around on, but they are often combined into larger ensembles as well. Rice farmers are said to have invented them as a way to keep idle fingers busy while resting in some shady spot away from the midday sun. Visitors to Bali often hear tingklik performed as background music in hotels and restaurants. Yet despite these casual associations, there is a rich repertoire of music for them.

Balinese *suling* (flutes) are universally made of bamboo. They are end blown from a nodal point in the tube, with a little hole cut in to allow the breath to pass through the resonating chamber. Fingering holes are bored along the length of the instrument. The husky *suling gambuh* is the longest, with all sizes available down to a piercing little *suling kantilan* that can be heard through the texture of the loudest orchestral passages. Suling are always played with circular breathing, a difficult technique whereby the flutist exhales air stored in the cheeks while inhaling through the nose. This makes it possible for the flute to sound continuously.

The instruments described above are the most frequently encountered in Bali, but the list is far from complete. Bali is peppered with all sorts of unusual music-making tools. The bowed rebab, already mentioned in connection with *gamelan gambuh* (see Chapter Two), finds its way into many ceremonial ensembles. It is much loved for the dignified tone it imparts when well-played. The sound of a poorly played rebab, though, has been compared by some Balinese to the squeals of a pig being slaughtered at feast time!

Other instruments include the *genggong* (a jaw harp), the *guntang*, (a bamboo slit drum that functions as a gong), the *preret* (a reedy trumpet heard in East Bali and Lombok), and many other ingenious devices made from simple and readily available materials. The panoply of Balinese musical instruments runs the gamut from the sophisticated construction of the gongs and metallophones down to such simple objects as a piece of bamboo and a stick. All find their way into the world of Balinese music.

CHAPTER FOUR

Basic Principles of Gamelan Music

To investigate the way that a music works is to uncover the manner in which the musicians and composers in a particular tradition express themselves and their culture. At their disposal is their own creative power, consideration of the uses to which the music will be put, and the possibilities suggested by the musical instruments that they possess. They are bounded by the limits of their experience and what their culture accepts or deems artistically suitable. The act of composing music is the act of ordering and patterning the flow of time; hence the way that the musicians in a society choose to do this says quite a lot about their philosophical perspective and aesthetic outlook. Music teaches humanity about time and its many kinds of flow.

Conveying the elusive nature of time has always been an Achilles heel of language, which is why in most languages metaphors of space are used. We speak of musical lines, intervals, moving forward, up and down the scale, and so on, and are so used to these visualizations that they are unremarkable. In much of Western music, time in general has been conceived of as linear, moving like a line from one "place" to the next. A composition begins, proceeds, its themes are elaborated upon, and it ends, all in a continuously unfolding process in which repetition (which could turn a line into a circle) is masked. While certain melodies or sections may be repeated during the course of a work, they are just as likely to return in a changed form as not. This is part of what makes the music challenging and satisfying to follow. The Western musical aesthetic, in turn, might be correlated with wider cultural notions about progress, development and change.

Time in Balinese *gamelan*, like many other musics throughout the world, has most often been characterized as cyclic or regenerative—notably by the Balinese themselves. That is to say the music normally returns repeatedly to the same 'point', like a planet in orbit or the hands on a clock. A cycle is formed in such a way that the last note of a melody is also the first note of its recurrence, as though a circle was being drawn and the final arc closed. That moment of renewal is of primary importance and is signified by a stroke of the large gong. Perhaps, as was suggested in Chapter Two, this reflects the importance of reincarnation in Hindu belief. Possibly it symbolizes an attachment to the harvest cycles that have supported agriculture on Bali's soil for centuries, providing them with an abundance of food that led them to develop feasts and rituals to celebrate. In any case, most gamelan compositions are strengthened through immediate repetition of their various internal sections. Yet cycles never recur without different kinds of change and variation built-in too, so repetition is never *merely* repetition.

The so-called circular temporal duration that passes between two gong strokes is filled in with a variety of melodies and rhythms. Perhaps the most important of these is the slow, measured line of the two 5-keyed *calung*, stressed occasionally by the pair of deep-toned *jegogan*, which comprise the "core" melody. All other aspects of the music—the rhythmic variations, shifts in tempo and intensity, and the impressionistic changes of color—owe their allegiance to this basic tune, which can be heard sailing placidly through the middle and lower registers of the ensemble. Other elements in the music may transform rapidly and unpredictably, but the core melody and the gong are the dependable safeguards of cyclical time.

Since the music is orchestral in conception it follows that there are many different musical parts. Each part is related in a specific way to the core melody and the gong and can be derived from or traced to them with ease by an experienced musician. In traditional repertoires the different kinds of musical parts do not vary very much between pieces and are usually executed by the same groups of instruments. Thus every instrument in the ensemble has a precisely prescribed role to play in making up the whole—a fleshing out of the musical curve carved out between the soundings of the gong, and a richly detailed set of variations on that single, core melodic line.

In our description of gamelan music it will be helpful to divide the instruments of the ensemble into two groups—those that play the core melody or some sort of variation on it, and those that describe the melody's form or shape. Thus the former group, consisting of the jegogan, calung, *gangsa*, *suling*, *rebab*, *trompong* and *reyong* (in short, all of the tuned instruments) provide the melodic content of the music. The latter group, headed by the large gong and including its smaller siblings the *kempur* and *klentong*, the time-beater *kempli* (or *kajar*), the *cengceng*, and the two *kendang*, furnish a framework for the melody. Every instrument in the gamelan, like every member of the community in preparation for a temple ritual, has a crucial role to play.

Instruments that Trace the Form

Just about all gamelan music is grounded by a large gong to mark the beginnings and endings of melodies and a kempli or kajar to keep a steady beat. Musicians are so dependent on the reassuring sound of these two instruments that if their players are ever absent from a rehearsal confusion is bound to ensue. In between the strokes of the large gong, the smaller gongs find their places—different places depending on the type of melody. The form of the melody is therefore delineated by 1) the number of kempli beats between two strokes of the large gong, and 2) the particular pattern of strokes of the lesser gongs. This technique of using gongs to define the form was dubbed *colotomy* (from the Greek *colon,* meaning arm or limb) by Dutch musicologist Jaap Kunst; the arrangement of gongs within a melody is referred to as the colotomic structure. Balinese call them *gongan*.

Gongan range in length from 2 kempli beats to broad canvasses of 256. In general the shorter the pattern the more it is repeated within a composition. The warm sound of the kempur and the contrasting sharp peal of the klentong, appearing within the cycle at crucial points, furnish a set of musical signs that enhance the power of the return to gong. They are almost always placed in such a way as to divide the cycle into even sections of 2, 4, 8, 16, or 32 beats. The sense of expectation engendered by such equal time divisions makes the arrival of the final gong a very satisfying event, especially after one of the longer patterns.

Playing the kempli is a skill that requires admittedly little instrumental dexterity, yet it demands a complete and thorough understanding of the music and an awareness of fine shadings of tempo. The beat of the kempli sustains and coordinates the ensemble, scouting out upcoming changes in speed and adjusting the beat accordingly without rocking the boat too much. Musicians unconsciously look to it to fit their rhythms into place. In rare instances where the ensemble's coordination threatens to unravel, the players' eyes and ears will hone in immediately on the kempli's beat seeking clarification, and the kempli player is expected to provide it in no uncertain terms.

To get a feeling for one of the most characteristic colotomic structures, try studying, and then singing or clapping, the 16-beat phrase notated below at a comfortable speed. The key underneath explains the symbols and sounds used. This pattern is known as *gegaboran;* it is found underlying melodies in a variety of female dances related to the offering dance *gabor,* and also in instrumental music.

GONGS:	**G**			**P**				**T**				**P**				**G**
KEMPLI:	K	K	K	K	K	K	K	K	K	K	K	K	K	K	K	K
BEAT#:	1	2	3	4	5	6	7	8	9	10	11	12	13	14	15	16 (1)
SING:	*Gir*	*tuk*	*tuk*	*tuk*	**Pur**	*tuk*	*tuk*	*tuk*	**Tong**	*tuk*	*tuk*	*tuk*	**Pur**	*tuk*	*tuk*	*tuk* **Gir**

Key:

Name	Symbol	Sung Syllable and Pronunciation
Gong	**G**	**Gir** *(sung on a low pitch, like English 'gear' with a rolled 'r')*
Kempur	**P**	**Pur** *(sung on a medium pitch, like English 'poor' with a rolled 'r')*
Klentong	**T**	**Tong** *(sung on a high pitch to rhyme with English 'long')*
Kempli	**K**	**Tuk** *(half-sung with a nasal sound, like English 'took')*

(The 'tuk' sound is dropped if it coincides with one of the other gongs.)

There are a wealth of different gongan structures used in Balinese music. Most conjure up a specific connotation for Balinese listeners, not unlike the way major and minor scales carry general emotional associations in

The two *kendang* control the ensemble, the *kempli* monitors the tempo,
the *ugal* carries the lead melody.

Western music. The gegaboran form noted on page 50, for example, will always bring with it the affect of a ritual female dance, even if it supports a melody for a purely abstract and instrumental composition. Likewise there are gong patterns that tend to call forth warlike sentiments, regal splendor, spiritual refinement and other responses. These feelings are further enhanced and modified by several factors, including the note of the scale with which the stroke of the large gong coincides, the tunings of the gongs in relation to the gamelan's scale (some gamelan's gongs match one of the pitches in its scale, others' fall completely outside of it), and the tuning of the gamelan as a whole.

The Core Melody and its Variants
The core melody and its variants fit snugly with the gongan. The tuned instruments each have their own parts, organized in levels so that the higher the pitch of the instrument the more complex the music it is called upon to play. In this stratified arrangement very stately sustained tones are relegated to the jegogan, a singing midrange line (the core melody itself) is played by the calung, the *ugal* and the trompong play a developed version of the

When playing *kotekan*, the musicians' mallets move up and down in coordinated alternation.

calung part, and the rest of the instruments fill the upper register with a shower of high speed ornamental figuration called *kotekan*. This arrangement is often metaphorically compared with a tree, where the core melody is represented by the trunk, the ugal and trompong by the limbs and branches, and the kotekan by the flowers or leaves. As with the gongan structure, the relationship between the parts is usually based on simple duple ratios. The kotekan instruments move 4 or 8 times faster than the calung and the ugal, which in turn play 2, 4, or 8 times faster than the jegogan. The busy chattering of the kotekan is solidly supported by the mellifluous tones and booming gongs below it.

Usually, the core melody is sounded by the calung at the rate of one tone per one or two kempli beats, although sometimes, especially in contemporary music, it is given more shape and not restricted to such a uniform rhythm. The jegogan are similarly regular, stressing the important notes of the calung line by simply doubling them on their keys, which sound an octave below. The jegogan also unfailingly coincide with the gongs, as if anchoring the core melody to the foundation provided by the colotomic instruments. At the ends of melodies, when the large gong, jegogan and calung all play together, the resultant sound, enhanced by the gamelan's

A good *trompong* player can communicate the richness of the *lelambatan* repertoire.

paired tuning, is very physical in its effect. Playing in the group or listening close by, the vibrations can be felt as well as heard.

Especially in older music, the core melody is usually too plain in itself to be particularly tuneful; its function is to proceed dependably like a sturdy walking bass in a jazz combo. In the registers above it, its tones are ornamented by the numerous melody instruments that it supports. The most flowing, singable version of the core melody tones—the ones a Balinese would sing if asked for their version of the 'main' melody of a given piece—is often buried in the middle of the texture on the tones of the ugal. This role falls also to the elegant trompong in older pieces; there it is much more prominent. Ugal and trompong each have their own distinctive style for ornamenting the core melody tones, connecting them to each other with syncopated curves and graceful melodic loops that always end up just where they should when final gong arrives.

Since the ugal and the trompong are generally not paired, and are therefore not coordinated note-for-note with any other musicians, their players are allowed some flexibility in interpreting the melody. This flexibility imparts a certain sense of fluidity and openness to the music. The skill with which these parts are executed greatly affects the feeling for the rest of the ensemble, so these instruments are entrusted to players of great skill. Their roles are among the few places where improvisation, albeit within a narrow range, can play a role in Balinese music. The suling and rebab, when present, also interpret the core melody in an improvisatory style, adding a much-desired sweetness of tone. But their presence is optional, whereas the music cannot possibly be played properly without the ugal, and in some cases the trompong.

Kotekan

The busy upper registers of the gamelan are the domain of the gangsa and reyong. These instruments spin out kotekan, the crackling ornamental fireworks of Balinese music. Kotekan is usually expressed in English as 'interlocking parts', because although it sounds as one melody it is actually composed of two interdependent musical lines that are incomplete when played alone and dependent exclusively on each other for obtaining the desired result. That can range from stately murmuring in some of the older, simpler styles of kotekan, to extroverted, jazzy acrobatics in modern music. The tight interaction of the two parts produces a supple texture that is pointillistic in detail and fluid as a whole.

The two components of kotekan are termed *polos* and *sangsih.* The polos is derived from the core melody and coincides with it from time to time, while the sangsih complements the polos by filling in any rhythmic gaps in its structure. From the two parts' interaction, a motoric steady stream of melody emerges. In some kinds of kotekan this means that the polos simply plays a regular succession of two notes per kempli beat. The sangsih interlocks with this by playing right in-between the polos tones; together they divide the beat into four equal parts. In other kinds both polos and sangsih are composed of syncopated rhythms which complement each other ingeniously. In such cases the two parts occasionally coincide at the unison or some sonorous interval. This produces irregular accents that bubble up from the flow of the kotekan's melody, dancing skittishly around the smooth beat of the kempli. Much of the excitement of Balinese music arises from these irresistible rhythms.

A very common and straightforward kind of kotekan is called *norot* (or *nuutin),* which means 'following' in Balinese. In it, the polos rests comfortably on the same tones as the core melody, striking twice per beat and moving to a new note only when the core melody does. The sangsih fits in between, repeating the next-highest tone in the scale. The result, diagrammed below, is like a slow trill or rocking back-and-forth between the two parts. In performance one can see the polos and sangsih players' mallets moving up and down in coordinated alternation.

```
Sangsih tones:    S    S    S    S    S    S    S    S
Polos tones:    P    P    P    P    P    P    P    P
Calung tones:   C –  –  –  –  –  –  – C –  –  –  –  –  –  –      etc.
Jegogan tones:  J –  –  –  –  –  –  –  –  –  –  –  –  –  –  –
Kempli beat:    K         K         K         K
```

A more syncopated type of kotekan, in which the polos and sangsih coincide every few notes, could be represented like this:

```
Sangsih tones:    S S    S S S    S    S S    S S
Polos tones:    P    P P    P    P P P    P P    P P
Calung tones:   C –  –  –  –  –  –  – C –  –  –  –  –  –  –      etc.
Jegogan tones:  J –  –  –  –  –  –  –  –  –  –  –  –  –  –  –
Kempli beat:    K         K         K         K
```

Notice that in both examples every part of the beat is filled with either a polos or sangsih tone, or both.[1]

An enormous variety of kotekan have been created and new ones are being invented all the time. They provide endless beguilement for gamelan musicians and are a showcase for the talents of their composers. But too much complexity is wearing for the listener, so kotekan is not employed exclusively. Sometimes the upper registers ring out with bold and strikingly profiled unison passages that provide welcome contrast—and give the players' tired hands a break! Moreover, kotekan is most effective at quick tempos, where the rhythmic excitement finds its most comfortable gait. At slow speeds, languid melodies often weave through the texture. Sometimes it is slow enough for both parts of the kotekan to be handled by a single player; this imbues the patterns with an entirely different, more

---

1 In the next chapter, a complete *kotekan* pattern will be discussed in detail.

relaxed character. A balanced diet of slow and fast, some kotekan and some unison passages, is considered essential in any piece.

But playing kotekan at the unimaginable speeds that some gamelan attain requires terrific coordination, a flawless instrumental technique, and musicality sensitive enough to respond to the precise, unmistakable 'click' of polos and sangsih settling into their complementary rhythmic niches. The sensation of being locked in with another part, racing through a melody in a breathless rhythmic embrace, is an epiphany unlike any other musical experience in the world.

Role of the Drums

The two kendang that direct the gamelan play elaborate patterns that are like kotekan. The higher pitched lanang (see page 44) is roughly comparable to the polos—its rhythms generally align with those of the kempli. The deeper *wadon*'s part is composed to fall in between. Together they produce phrases that move at or near the speed of the kotekan. In addition to negotiating these complexities, one of the drummers is also responsible for coordinating the entire gamelan's changes of speed and volume, for interpreting any cues that a dancer may give, and for signaling the beginnings and endings of sections.[2] For these reasons among others, many consider the kendang to be the most difficult instrument in the gamelan. This is partly because of the dexterity, endurance and strength required to master the technique of playing, but also because a drummer must understand all aspects of the music and know all of the other parts exhaustively in order to be a competent director. Almost invariably drummers lead rehearsals and create new compositions too, making them even more indispensable.

In certain kinds of music, notably the Jauk and Barong masked dances, the music moves too swiftly and the changes come too abruptly for participation by a pair of drummers to be practical. In such cases the lead kendang player takes over alone and plays in a virtuoso, improvisatory manner. The repertoire of rhythmic patterns on which to improvise is broad and drummers delight in collecting them, inventing them and putting them together

---

2   Whether it is the *wadon* or the *lanang* that fulfills this function depends on the type of music. In the *gamelan gong kebyar* the wadon is usually the leader, but for certain music, notably the male dance forms and masked dances, the lanang takes over. The lanang also has a primary role in the older styles *gambuh*, *semar pegulingan* and *pelegongan.*

The drummer mediates between dancer and gamelan by being watchful and alert to cues.

in different combinations. The best players develop a very personal style over the course of their careers, acquiring signature phrases and rhythmic tricks that are designed to baffle would-be emulators and give a distinctive mark to their playing.

Perhaps the highest compliment that a drummer can receive is that his playing is *suba ela*—that is, completely natural and easy, despite the intricacies of the rhythms. The best *kebyar* drummers 'dance' while they play, using their torsos, arms, hands and facial expressions to help express the music, show the degree to which they have mastered it, and to add drama to the performance. In older styles of music, a more reserved demeanor is considered appropriate.

The experience of performing on the lead kendang in a Balinese gamelan is one of exhilaration and responsibility. All members of the group seek clarification and reassurance that the music is proceeding as it should by listening carefully for important drum cues and by establishing eye contact with the drummer when possible. The drummer must be fluent enough with his part that most of his energy can be directed towards monitoring the group, constantly checking to make sure that things don't go awry. If there is a dancer, the kendang acts as intermediary, translating key dance movements into musical impulses with deftly placed strokes that send messages in a flash to the ensemble. The lead drummer communicates the essence of the music in sound, bearing and gesture.

Tempo, Dynamics, and Other Subtleties

Balinese musicians speak of ensemble feeling as a fundamental aspect of any performance. Executing the core melody, gong strokes, melodic variations and drum patterns with mere correctness is only the first step in playing a piece of music. Any group worth its salt must also master the spirit and nuance of a composition, knowing just when to speed up or slow down, when to get loud and when to get soft, and whether to do so suddenly or gradually. The music and the musicians must breathe together; they must *majiwai gending:* feel the soul of the music as one.

The prime aesthetic criterion for a good gamelan performance is that of tight ensemble coordination. In order to achieve this every part is carefully composed, memorized, and then practiced again and again until its execution is a matter of reflex and instinct. Consequently, although there are a few limited contexts for improvisation in Balinese music (as mentioned above) the point of this is to add unpredictable colors to the sound here and there—but it is not considered as individual expression by any means. The goal is instead to achieve complete mastery of a given piece of music and to play it to perfection together with the rest of the ensemble. While playing, each musician listens attentively and is aware not only of his or her individual part, complex as it may be, but also of its relationship to the whole and especially to the core melody. Soloists emerge rarely; instead each member of the gamelan tries to be precisely coordinated with the others, like a vital part of a single living organism.

Change of tempo originates with the signals of the ugal and kendang players and is regulated by the careful increase or decrease in the rate of kempli strokes, all of which must be alertly followed by the rest of the group. Plenty of practice is needed to perfect the suspenseful, gradual accelerations and ritardandos that are such a hallmark of the music. The effect of 25 or more musicians changing speed in perfect synchronization is very impressive indeed, especially when one takes into account the difficulty of keeping kotekan rhythms interlocked even at a steady pace. Sometimes, notably at transition points or endings, the tempo leaps to a higher or lower level very suddenly. In such cases, the players must memorize the sensation of playing at both tempi and be able to switch from one to the other with ease.

There is great sensitivity to gradations of loud and soft in Balinese music. The wide dynamic capacity of the instruments is thoroughly exploited with both subtle and violent changes in volume. Often extremes of dynamic are juxtaposed to create an atmosphere of tension and unpredictability. Cues for such changes are given by the ugal player, who indicates the dynamic of an upcoming passage by raising his mallet. The higher it goes, the louder the subsequent section will be. These changes are never decided extemporaneously, however, but are planned at rehearsals and specified note-for-note.

The music also finds expression in the palette of tonal colors available and through the contrasts that are achieved by bringing out the sound of a particular group of instruments. A repeating melody may be enlivened by having the gangsa play louder than the rest for a few cycles, followed perhaps by turns for the suling, kendang, calung and reyong. The spectrum of sound shifts gradually as one group fades out and another emerges. Sometimes a section of the gamelan drops out altogether for a time, revealing a sparser, more translucent texture.

Often the steady flow of drums, melody and kotekan is rocked by a sharp, syncopated accent called *angsel*. This term originates with the dance, where it refers to a sudden movement which is mimicked in like rhythm by the gamelan. But angsel are a crucial agent for rhythmic variety in instrumental music too. They are always preceded by a few beats with cues from the kendang and/or the ugal. At the right moment—usually just prior to the gong—the kendang, cengceng, gangsa and reyong converge on the angsel rhythm. But the gongs and core melody continue ineluctably, undisturbed by the commotion around them.

Form and Composition

Musical form in Balinese music runs the gamut from short pieces made up of a single repeating melody to multi-movement works of symphonic breadth and scope. In older music, the form is determined by the structure of the gongan—that is, a piece of music is classified and named according to the pattern of gongs marking it. Modern pieces may be freer and more fantasia-like, concatenating a succession of rhapsodic melodies, or even introducing passages that involve no gong punctuation at all.

Ostinati (short, repeating melodies) are important in processional music and for accompanying many male dance forms. They also appear as stirring finales to lengthy ceremonial pieces and in any dance or theatrical setting where a brisk, martial mood is appropriate. By far the most common gong pattern for ostinati is the *gilak,* an 8, 16 or 32-beat structure that features two kempur strokes aligned towards the end of the cycle in a peculiarly asymmetrical way. They seem to make the music fall headlong into the gong that follows, as if pulled in by gravitational forces. If the gamelan has one, a second large gong, somewhat smaller than the main one but still weighty enough in sound to contribute substantial power, is used to mark the middle of the cycle. The 8-beat gilak, with large gongs on beats 1 and 5 and kempur on beats 6 and 8, can be notated as follows:

Gongs & Kempur:	G				G	P		P	G	
Kempli beats:		K	K	K	K	K	K	K	K	K	*etc.*
Beat #:		1	2	3	4	5	6	7	8	1

The form of the music is delineated by the pattern of gong strokes.

Listen for the dense pulsations of gilak in the *gamelan baeganjur* (also called *bebonangan),* the ensemble of gongs, kendang and cengceng used in processions. The urgent excitement it generates adds a great deal to the atmosphere at such occasions. Other important ostinati encountered in Balinese music are the aforementioned gegaboran, associated with female dances, the *bapang,* used in *jauk* and other choreographies, and the *batel,* common in dramatic contexts for accompanying fight scenes.

At the other end of the spectrum are the majestic long forms that comprise the heart of the classical repertoire. In the temple at ceremony time, one gamelan usually holds forth with *lelambatan* (lit: slow music) for the pleasure of the visiting deities. Here Balinese music reaches its zenith of structural development with long and complex compositions that take up to 45 minutes to perform. Adapted from the repertoire of the *gamelan gong gdé* of the courts, these pieces are distinguished by the presence of the trompong and the boom of kendang played with mallets; they are also accompanied by the constant clash of the giant *cengceng kopyak.* The sheer weightiness of the sound of lelambatan gives a good indication of its significance.

A lelambatan usually opens with an austere and meditative introduction for trompong (suling and rebab are often present as well), punctuated sparely with pulsating jegogan tones. The rich resonances of the trompong's tones and the graceful melodic ornaments supplied by the player reach deep into the melody, bringing forth a wealth of musical feeling. Soon the drums enter and, following quickly, the rest of the gamelan. The ensuing phrases explore a variety of textures and tempi, often previewing melodic ideas that are slated for a role later on. After a time the trompong and drums emerge again, heralding the *pengawak,* or main movement.

There are 8 varieties of *lelambatan pengawak,* named and distinguished from each other by their length and colotomic structure. The simplest is *tabuh pisan (tabuh* = composition; *pisan* = one), which usually consists of eight melodic phrases of 16 beats, bisected and finished with strokes of the large gong. Other types of lelambatan pengawak form involve the kempur and also the kempli, whose role is altered from that of beat-keeper. Among them, *tabuh kutus (kutus* = 8) is the broadest. Here, kempli and kempur strokes alternate, separated from each other by 16 beat phrases, until each has sounded eight times. When gong finally arrives, 256 beats have elapsed—a considerable time and musical distance (see diagram on right).

_____ P	_____
_____ K	_____
_____ P	_____
_____ K	_____ G
_____ P	_____
_____ K	_____
_____ P	_____
_____ K	_____ G
_____ P	
_____ K	*Form for tabuh pisan (1) pengawak*
_____ P	
_____ K	
_____ P	
_____ K	
_____ P	
_____ G	

Form for tabuh kutus (8) pengawak

Key: K = Kempli
P = Kempur
G = Gong
Each line = 16 beats

Of the eight forms, tabuh types 1, 3 and 4 are the most common. Among different compositions within each type, the melodies are always different and there is some flexibility as to how the totality is constructed. But the gong and drumming patterns for the pengawak section are constant from piece to piece. Individual lelambatan are referred to by their pengawak type and a given name. For instance, *tabuh nem Galang Kangin (nem* = 6) means "Eastern Sunlight: type six lelambatan composition."

The pengawak is majestic in tempo and may be repeated 3 or 4 times in a temple performance. Often the atmosphere in the temple is so informal that the musicians take coffee and cigarette breaks between repetitions! Actually they are in a kind of holding pattern, waiting for indications that the ceremony is about to intensify. When the flow of offerings being carried to and from the inner courtyards is bustling and the priests begin chanting the sacred ceremonial rites, the trompong player cues the musicians on to a series of other movements which build slowly in speed and excitement while growing proportionately shorter in length. This telescoping of musical energy is timed to synchronize with the progress of the rituals. Usually by the final section the scope of the composition has been reduced to that of an ostinato, which brings the piece to a thundering conclusion. As the tones of the lelambatan fade away they are supplanted by other sonic activity: the sweet-toned *gamelan angklung* (which often plays right across the courtyard), groups of women singing ancient *kidung* songs, loudspeaker announcements, the barking of vendors on the street outside, and the gossamer tinkling of the high priests' bells.

Lelambatan melodies are subtle and restrained, using mainly simpler types of ornament and kotekan. What may at first seem to be a rather flat and monotonous texture reveals itself upon repeated listening to be a rich trove of inventiveness and Balinese musical feeling. These are the pieces closest to the hearts of most Balinese. They hear them regularly in the temple from childhood on, and associate their dignified demeanor with the rarefied spiritual world that they encounter there.

Other Ensembles, Other Forms

In the compositions that comprise the repertoire of the ancient *gamelan gambuh* and its direct descendants *gamelan semar pegulingan* and *gamelan pelegongan*, a variety of musical forms have evolved. Many of the colotomic structures used resemble those in lelambatan, but in these delicate styles the large gong is replaced by the kempur and the kempur defers to the bright sound of the klentong. In really authentic versions, the flat-bossed kajar unseats the kempli, tapping along in tandem with the patter of the small kendang used rather than simply stating the beat. A suite of melodies for the *legong*, the much-beloved series of classical Balinese choreographies for young girls, opens with a lengthy prelude—the dance of the *condong,* or court attendant. The condong's dance is based on a series of ostinati that are interspersed and repeated with variations in tempo, ornamentation, and angsel. Thereupon follows a medium-sized pengawak and a number of shorter movements arranged according to the particular legong story portrayed. It has become acceptable to omit some of the longer melodies in performances of legong in order to shorten the performance; hopefully this will not diminish appreciation of the complete versions, which are magnificent compositions and should be preserved in full.

Musical structures in other kinds of gamelan are faithful to the basic principles of cyclical structure and core melody with variations, but they vary greatly within that context, sometimes becoming wildly asymmetrical or irregular. Compositions for the *gamelan gender wayang* may be associated with specific scenes or characters in the shadow play or underpin the puppeteer's singing. The instrumental pieces for this gamelan are jewels of labyrinthine melodies and kotekan. The 4-tone gamelan angklung that is often heard in the temples makes the most of its tiny range with its own special kotekan style, nestled into colotomic patterns of often odd and unpredictable lengths. The bamboo-keyed *gamelan joged bumbung* and *gamelan jegog*, tremendously popular in the western part of the island, adapt some of their music from popular songs.

A few older gamelan with wholly sacred uses base, in part, their formal structures on verse forms in classical poetry, which has always been sung. In voicing poetry, the number of lines in the poem and the number of syllables in each line are used to determine the number of phrases in the melody. Further, in each type of verse form each line must end with a specified vowel sound. How did this get transferred to instrumental gamelan music? Although the evidence is inconsistent, some think the vowel sounds used in the poetry were at one time mapped on to the musical phrase to compose the melody itself: a, e, i, o and u in the text became *ding, dong, deng, dung, and dang* in the music.

Most of these gamelan have fixed repertoires that are tampered with only a little today, if at all. The 20th century saw dramatic changes in Balinese musical form, however. These had their beginnings in the '20s and '30s with the works of Lotring and his contemporaries. Lotring had a genius for constructing free-form works for the pelegongan and *kebyar gamelan* that vividly evoked other Balinese styles. His compositions Gambangan and Angklungan (based on the musics of the *gamelan gambang* and the gamelan angklung) lifted those styles out of their restricted ritual settings and made use of their melodies and rhythms in a secular, entertainment context. Lotring was especially expert at gamelan gender wayang. He modified many pieces from this style, transposing them from their original *slendro* into the *pélog* tuning that was his preferred compositional medium.

Lotring's work opened the door for other composers to rearrange, invent, alter and discard musical ideas and materials as it suited them, as long as the music they composed was intended for secular use. The sacred styles, then as now, remain intact. The *kreasi baru* (lit: new creations) music and dance compositions for the *gamelan gong kebyar* that appeared by the hundreds during the following decades were freely composed, eclectic and novel, often emphasizing the virtuosity of the musicians and flashy new styles of kotekan. By the late 1970s, though, this excess of freedom had been allowed to degenerate into cliché.

Composers of the 1980s and '90s recognized this and remedied the situation in several ways. One was to refine and extend the existing kreasi baru style. Another was to return to composing in older forms. A third way has been to invent new instrumental techniques and combinations or even new instruments. This last group has produced some brilliant and intriguing new ideas. Komang Astita, a musician from Denpasar, composed Eka Dasa Rudra, using several gamelan at once to evoke the gorgeous cacophony of the massive centennial ceremony of the same name that was held at Besakih temple in 1979. Other composers playfully used such objects as kitchen utensils, rocks and brooms in their whimsical and energetic work of those years. This experimental genre became known as *musik kontemporer*, and, as will be shown in Chapter Ten, its practitioners have continued to push beyond the mainstream of the tradition

There are few limits on what is acceptable or possible in Balinese music today. The accelerated pace of life on the island is reflected in the broadening of what the culture as a whole accepts as artistically viable. Composers and their music are as susceptible to these changes as any other segment of the society; this naturally has resulted in the rapid development of untried and unusual musical forms. Most of these will not have any impact beyond the excitement of their initial performances, but a few will stick. Recent music reflects the new approaches to aesthetics and the new artistic liberties that are part of Balinese life now.

CHAPTER FIVE

The Music for
the Baris Dance

Initial encounters with music as foreign to Western ears as Balinese *gamelan* are understandably bewildering to most. Even for sensitive and sympathetic listeners it is difficult to make much sense of the music until after repeated exposure to the new sounds, instruments and tunings. The problem is compounded by the fact that the music is orchestral and so much is happening at once. Some sort of step-by-step guide that applies the abstract concepts presented in the previous chapter to a particular piece of music therefore seems worth pursuing.

The strategy will be to coach you in understanding, singing and playing all the different parts for one short composition, using the same sounds and syllables that a Balinese musician would if they were not playing on the actual instruments. Our tools will be the first two tracks on the book CD, plus your own participation singing on the four notes *do, mi, fa, sol* (skipping *re*) of the Western major scale, a steady foot tap or hand clap, a robust (and not necessarily beautiful) singing voice, and a little time and patience. Those with greater musical aptitude may do better on the complex elaborations than others, but do not let this daunt you. All of the parts are important and a facility with any of them will reward you with increased appreciation of the music. If you are in Bali, ask a musician to help you if you can. He or she may well be delighted by your interest.

The discussion will be limited to a detailed description of the music for the Baris dance, as played on the standard *gamelan gong kebyar* tuned to 5-tone *pélog*. The modern solo Baris is a dance form with its roots in antiquity. The word itself means row, rank or file and actually refers to a whole family of choreographies that portray martial and warlike characters. Most of these were originally for companies of dancers bearing lances or shields; the group forms still extant today are mainly sacred and seen only at special ceremonies. The solo dance, however, has been distilled and secularized. Today it can be seen on the program at many recreational performances, whether as entertainment for Balinese outside a temple during a ceremony or as part of a tourist show.

While the older ritual Baris forms are comprised of relatively plain choreographies, the execution of the more intricate modern one (which has the full name Baris Melampahan) requires intensive practice and consummate skill. Most male and many female dance students begin their training with this dance, as it develops the most important musculature, movements and postures in the Balinese dance vocabulary. Since the dancer may in effect vary the order of the larger gestures of the choreography during the course of a performance, a Baris performer must have complete understanding of the musical accompaniment too, as he is required to instantiate these gestures at precisely the proper moment in the course of the music. In contemporary Baris the dancer leads the gamelan, carrying the musicians along through a succession of sharply drawn moods and vignettes that illustrate the warrior's alternately watchful and combative states.

Beryl De Zoete and Walter Spies, writing in *Dance and Drama in Bali* (Faber and Faber Ltd., London, 1938, p. 168), give the following evocative description of the Baris' character: "The evolutions of this dance can be of intense brilliance: the fierce darting glance, the neck movements so swift that they seem like a trill of sound; the leaps, the wheeling flight; the restless splendor of glittering crest and swinging stoles; ... the sudden smile, infinitely alluring; the narrowed eyelids lifted to reveal blazing balls of darkness set in a shining rim. Sometimes a lightning pirouette will lift in a whirl of color the short brilliant stoles which hang thick as feathers on his back. The Baris dance has an undeniable fighting bird quality."

Baris is usually 10 to 12 minutes long. The music and the dance are in three parts, each of which are based on 8-beat *gongan*. The first and last parts are quite similar to each other, while the central section is wholly unrelated. We shall concern ourselves with the first part only. The intent is to give as complete a picture as possible of what is happening in the music and how it is connected to the dance through words, diagrams, notations and photographs.

Before we proceed, a pair of disclaimers. Baris has been chosen for our purposes because it is one of the most ubiquitous pieces of music in Bali. In spite of the brevity of its melody it contains all of the elements found in more developed pieces. But because it is so common there is also regional variation in performing it, so that the version discussed in the following pages may differ a bit from the one you chance to hear in performance or on a recording. These discrepancies, however, can only be at the level of minor detail; the various parts set forth herein will unquestionably be identifiable as parts of Baris to any Balinese, even though they may not coincide exactly with the way it is performed in his or her village.

Secondly, there is the matter of tempo. Baris, like much Balinese music, is played impossibly fast. Attempting to follow music moving at such breakneck speeds can be very frustrating since it requires a vigilant and unwavering concentration as well as a thorough familiarity with the materials, especially when it comes to the *kotekan* and *kendang* parts. Practice what is given here slowly until you can execute it well, but prepare for a shock when you listen again to a performance. The musicians will invariably play faster than you can think! Of course, the players themselves are *not* thinking, rather they are repeating gestures that they have practiced together thousands of times. After a while you will be able to follow them. In the meantime, imagine the thrill of doing something so fast and complex in coordination with so many others.

Our notation will be simple. The Balinese solfège syllables (see page 37) will be used to indicate the tones in the melodic parts. In the notations beginning on page 73, each musical line will be written across the page and shown above and in relation to the pattern of gongs and *kempli* in the cycle. Next to each notation will be a sketch of the instrument that it is played on, with the specific gongs or keys used in Baris darkened in.

A word about the configuration of gongs and keys on the instruments: we have seen that *ding, dong, deng, dung* and *dang* of a five-tone pélog tuning can be roughly compared to our *mi, fa, sol, ti, do,* or E-F-G-B-C. In the gamelan they are extended over a range of more than four octaves, with the tones divided among the instruments (in most instances) as shown below:

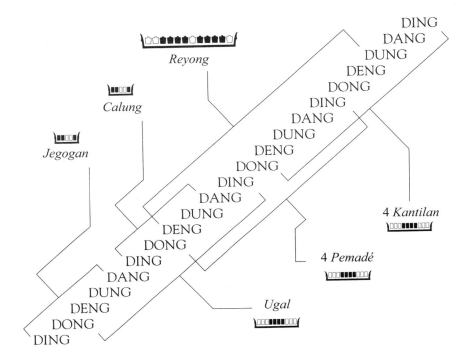

In addition to having different ranges, it is evident that the instruments also have individual arrangements of keys or gongs. The *jegogan* and *calung* cover only one octave, beginning on *ding* and ending on *dang*. The *ugal, pemadé* and *kantilan*, separated from each other by octaves, each begin on *dong* and stretch up ten notes to high *ding*. The span of the twelve small gongs of the reyong connects midrange *deng* with *dung* more than two octaves above. Hence, if all the players strike the note *deng* together, the calung and jegogan will hit their 3rd key, the *gangsa* their 2nd (or 7th), and the 1st, 6th and 11th *reyong* gongs will be played. Tunes that roam the full two octave range of the gangsa must be rearranged in order to squeeze the core tones into the single octave of the calung and jegogan. Thus even though it sometimes looks as though players' mallets are moving in opposite directions, they may actually be playing the same notes.

Introduction and Form

[All of the musical parts described in the following sections of the chapter can be heard individually and in combination, recorded at a specially slowed-down tempo, on track 1 of the book CD.]

Baris opens with an arresting kendang fanfare, usually performed solo in a fairly improvisatory style by the lead drummer playing on the higher-pitched *lanang* drum. The slapping sound produced by the left hand is called *pak*, and the deep pitch obtained from striking the right drumhead with a mallet is called *dug* (say: doog). Both may be used freely in a few declamatory opening phrases, but after a moment the following rhythm emerges, instantly recognized as a cue by the ensemble.

pak DUG pak DUG pak DUG DUG DUG DUG DUG DUG BYONG

The last group of six even *dug* strokes sets the tempo to come, one kempli beat for every two *dug*. Led by the raised mallet of the ugal player, the entire gamelan comes crashing down on the note *dang* right after the final drum stroke, making an explosive attack the Balinese call *byong*. After a few flourishes the large gong sounds, the kempli starts tapping the beat, the jegogan and calung enter, and the Baris melody proper begins.

The Baris ostinato is in *gilak* form (see page 60). From the sounding of the initial gong, the gongan pattern and core melody cycle continuously until the end.[1] Meanwhile, the rest of the instruments may be said to be in either a "stable" or an "active" state. In the former they are repeating prescribed patterns. In the latter they are somehow reacting to *angsel*—signals given by the dancer—by interrupting the flow of those patterns. The stable state is quiet, static and tense; the active state is explosive and kinetic. Moving from the former to the latter is a matter of sudden release and violent crescendo. When the dancer completes the angsel movement the activated instruments simply drop out and remain silent for a moment, leaving only the gongs, jegogan, and calung. Soon they reenter on their patterns as before.

---

1   There is one point at which the core melody does change; this will be taken up later.

Simple Melodic Parts

Once the introduction is over and the dancer has entered, we can count on the music to remain in the stable state for a few moments (on CD track 2, the performance version, this is the moment when the flute enters). This is a good time to focus on the various melodic parts. Don't attempt to hear all

Ritual Baris dancers, North Bali, circa 1857.

of them at once. Choose one and search for it in the texture with your ears. When you are satisfied that you have found it and can understand its relationship to the kempli and the gongs, move on to another part.

The most easily discernible melodic part is the tune played on the ugal and doubled both one and two octaves higher by the 4 pemadé and 4 kantilan. Of the ten keys available on these instruments, the melody uses only numbers 4, 5, 6, and 7. (Refer to the diagram on page 70.) These are the notes *dang, ding, dong,* and *deng* (On the piano: C, E, F and G/*do, mi, fa, sol*). In singing, however, the Balinese tend to replace the hard "d" sound with "n" or "nd," Hence *dang, ding, dong, deng* becomes *n(d)ang, n(d)ing, n(d)ong, n(d)eng*. The ugal part has a simple one tone per kempli beat relationship to the gong pattern.

The notation for the gilak, with the beats numbered 1 through 8 is the foundation upon which we shall lay the ugal part (and all the other parts in turn). The pitch *nang* should be used for gong and *neng* for kempur, but the syllables remain, as described in the previous chapter, *gir* for gong and *pur* for kempur. The *tuk* sound used for kempli need not have a specific pitch. The notation for the ugal and gongs is given below.

					neng					
UGAL:			nong			nong		nong		*etc.*
				ning					ning	
		nang					nang			nang
KEMPLI:	K	K	K	K	K	K	K	K	K	
GONG & KEMPUR:	G				G	P		P	G	
BEAT #:	1	2	3	4	5	6	7	8	1	

In the pemadé and kantilan version there are two mallet strokes per kempli beat. The melody is identical to the ugal's, with one small deviation—half of the players replace the note *nang* with *neng* whenever it occurs, as their coincidence creates a harmonious sound. This may be difficult to hear, but it does enrich the sound at those points. On the other pitches all play together.

	1	2	3	4	5	6	7	8	1	
	nengneng				nengneng	nengneng			neng	
PEMADÉ & KANTILAN:		nongnong			nongnong		nongnong			etc.
			ningning					ningning		
		nangnang					nangdnang		nang	
KEMPLI:	K	K	K	K	K	K	K	K	K	
GONG & KEMPUR:	G				G	P		P	G	
BEAT #:	1	2	3	4	5	6	7	8	1	

Next, the core melody itself. It comprises every other ugal tone beginning with the arrival of gong, except that the note on beat 7 is lowered to *ning* to give the line a smoother curve. Observe that because of the calung's limited 5-note range, we must choose a different configuration of keys. Instead of *nang* being the lowest note used, it is now the highest. This is simply because no other choice for that tone is available. In singing the line, raise *nang* one octave from the position it had earlier.

	1	2	3	4	5	6	7	8	1	
	nang								nang	
CALUNG:					nong					
			ning				ning			
KEMPLI:	K	K	K	K	K	K	K	K	K	etc.
GONG & KEMPUR:	G				G	P		P	G	
BEAT #:	1	2	3	4	5	6	7	8	1	

The jegogan are an octave deeper than the calung and play half as fast. As it turns out, the jegogan play together with the large gongs in Baris. Their slow rocking between *nang* and *nong* is like an axis on which the music turns. The order of the keys is identical to the calung.

	1	2	3	4	5	6	7	8	1	
	nang								nang	
JEGOGAN:					nong					
KEMPLI:	K	K	K	K	K	K	K	K	K	etc.
GONG & KEMPUR:	G				G	P		P	G	
BEAT#:	1	2	3	4	5	6	7	8	1	

Reyong Kotekan

After you are able to hear and identify these four parts, try to memorize them. If you have internalized the core melody and these simple variations on it, it will be much easier to relate them to the kotekan and drumming, which we shall take up next. When practicing these more complex parts, proceed slowly and break the line up into as many sub-units as necessary to facilitate your learning. Keep a steady beat with your foot or a hand clap, and always be aware of the connection between it and what you sing.

Recall first that kotekan consists of two interlocking parts, *polos* and *sangsih*, which fit together to make a single composite line. The resultant sequence of notes occurs at a rate of 4 tones per kempli beat, for a total of 32 in the complete Baris cycle. To clarify this in our notation, each kempli beat has been calibrated into four equal divisions. The interlocking parts for Baris are composed in such a way that there is little regularity in the way they fall amongst these divisions. Sometimes they coincide with the kempli strokes and other times they avoid them entirely. Because of these irregularities, it will be difficult to grasp the kotekan parts unless the four subdivisions of the beat are clearly demarcated in your mind's ear. They should tick along steadily like a little internal stopwatch.

The Baris kotekan is assigned to the four reyong players. Players 1 and 3 handle the polos, which is played entirely on the notes *dang* and *ding* (gongs number 3–4 and 8–9 for players 1 and 3 respectively), while the sangsih, naturally, is the responsibility of the other two musicians and is played on the tones *dong* and *deng* (gongs 5–6 and 10–11). The remaining gongs are not used. This configuration is diagrammed on pages 76–7.

Polos and sangsih are composed so that every note in their patterns lasts for either 1 subdivision (¼ beat) or 1 subdivision plus 1 subdivision of rest (a total of ½ beat). The interlocking occurs when one part sounds one of its tones at each instant that the other part is resting. This is how the continuous flow of notes is created.

To sing the parts, Balinese cut the final "ng" of the syllables when the kotekan note lasts for only ¼ beat. In other words, *nang, ning, nong* and *neng* sometimes become *na, ni, no,* and *ne*. Practice and memorize both parts, together with a friend if possible. This way when you know them you will be able to work on making them interlock together.

Notice further that the kotekan tones that coincide with the kempli are in

Beats	:	1	•	•	•	2	•	•	•	3	•	•	•
Reyong/Sangsih	:	ne'		neng		neng			ne'				
			no'		no'			nong		nong			
				ning		ning		ni'			ni'		
Reyong/Polos	:	nang	na'		na'			nang					
Ugal (*main melody*)	:	nang			nong			ning					
Calung (*core melody*)	:	nang						ning					
Kempli	:	K			K			K					
Gong & Kempur	:	G											
Kendang LH	:												
Lanang RH	:		dug	du'	dug	dug		dug		dug			
Kendang LH	:												
Wadon RH	:	dag	dag		dag	dag		dag		dag			

Notation of reyong and kendang parts, with gong, kempur, kempli and calung (core melody).

Beats (Clap)	:	1	•	•	•	2	•	•	•	3	•	•	•
Reyong/Polos	:	nang –		na'	ning –		na'	ning –		ni'	nang –		ni'

(*Key*: na' nang = do; ni', ning = mi)

Singing the reyong polos part alone

Beats (Clap)	:	1	•	•	•	2	•	•	•	3	•	•	•
Reyong/Sangsih	:	ne'	no'	neng –		no'	neng –		nong –		ne'	nong –	

(*Key*: no', nong = fa; ne', neng = sol)

Singing the reyong sangsih part alone

Beats (Clap)	:	1	•	•	•	2	•	•	•	3	•	•	•
Kendang	:		dag	dug	dag	du'	dug	dag	dug	dag	dug	dag	dug dag

Singing the composite drum part (for one person)

4 • • • **5** • • • **6** • • • **7** • • • **8** • • • • **1**

ne'   neng   ne'   ne'   ne'   ne'   ne'   neng
   no'   no'   nong   nong   nong   nong   nong
      ning   ni'   ni'   ni'   ni'   ni'   *etc.*

nang   na'   nang   nang   nang   nang   nang   nang

neng   nong   nang   nong   ning   nang

      nong   ning   nang

K   K   K   K   K   K
    G   P   P   G   *etc.*

    pak   pak   pak   pak   pak
dug   dug   dug   dug   dug

    kap   kap   kap   kap   kap
  da' dag   dag   dag   dag   dag

---

4 • • • **5** • • • **6** • • • **7** • • • **8** • • • • **1**

nang – na' ning – nang – ni' nang – ni' nang – ni' nang – ni' nang – ni' nang *etc.*

---

4 • • • **5** • • • **6** • • • **7** • • • **8** • • • • **1**

ne' no' neng – no' ne' nong – ne' nong – ne' nong – ne' nong – ne' nong – ne' *etc.*

---

4 • • • **5** • • • **6** • • • **7** • • • **8** • • • • **1**

dug da' dag dug dag pak kap dug dag pak kap pak kap dug dag pak kap pak kap dug dag *etc.*

Baris dancer: *seledet* (eye movement).

all cases the same as the ugal part at those points. It might therefore be said that the ugal tune is 'imbedded' in the kotekan, with the rest of the notes acting as decoration. Indeed, this is what is meant when the kotekan is referred to as elaboration of the main melody. Observe also that the outer notes *nang* and *neng* always sound together. In performance this means that the polos players' left hands and the sangsih players' right hands are synchronized. The interlocking can really be 'seen' in the interaction between the inner notes *ning* and *nong*, which are never struck at the same time. The coincidence of the outer tones, however, produces accents which emerge from the running line of the kotekan each time they are sounded, creating the aural sensation of an independent and irregular level of rhythm protruding from the texture. As you listen to the reyong in performance, try to zero in on this phenomenon. For an additional challenge, try to isolate those points of accent from the kotekan and sing them alone while tapping the beat.

Kendang Patterns

There are two different but closely related kendang patterns composed for Baris. One is used when the dancer is stationary or moving slowly, the other is for when the dancer steps briskly around the stage. The second one is given below the reyong notation on pages 76–7; it uses a greater variety of rhythms. The first, simpler one, will be derived from it presently.

As we noted when describing the kendang introduction to Baris, the higher-pitched lead kendang produces the sounds *pak* and *dug* with the left and right hands respectively. The former sounds like the dry crack of a whip and the latter, played with the mallet, a resonant bass. The deeper secondary drum requires the same technique to produce sounds that are equivalent but lower in pitch. On this drum *pak* is called *kap* and *dug* becomes *dag*. *Kap*, *pak*, *dug*, and *dag* are the only four drum sounds used in Baris.

The kendang's interlocking is conceptually similar to the *reyong kotekan*: one part fills in when the other rests. Unlike the reyong, though, the drum patterns never coincide. Instead, like sounds interact successively with like sounds, resulting in combinations like *kapakapak* and *dadugdadug*. (In singing quickly, as with kotekan, final consonants may be dropped.) When the dynamic is soft, the composite rhythm of the kendang sounds like a vague and expectant rumble, but when the music gets loud the swift exchanges crack and boom like thunder.

As with the kotekan, it is best to practice the drum parts with a friend in order to get the effect of the interlocking. In addition to singing them, try using the more percussive sounds obtained by substituting a handclap for *dag* and *dug* and a slap of the chest or thigh for *kap* and *pak*. As you build up to the complete pattern try working on just beats 1-4, repeating them cyclically. Just this much, played twice to fill a full eight-beat cycle, is the other, simpler, Baris kendang pattern mentioned above. Its resultant should sound as follows, with claps taking the place of *dag* and *dug* syllables as given.

—A—

	PLAYER 1 :	dug	du' dug	dug	dug	dug	dug		dug
	PLAYER 2 :	dag	dag		dag	dag	dag	dag	da' dag	dag

—B—

	KEMPLI	: K		K		K		K		K *etc.*
	BEAT#	: 1		2		3		4		1 (or 5)

Pay close attention to the "double" *dag* and *dug* strokes marked A and B above. These are the only places where the regular one-to-one alternation of

Preparing
angsel lantang.

Preparing
angsel bawak.

Executing
the *angsel.*

Finishing
the *angsel.*

Baris dancers' *angsel* movements.

strokes between the kendang is disturbed. The effect is to make the drums exchange positions with respect to the kempli beat, thereby adding extra energy and syncopation to the music. This also makes the patterns tougher to play, however, so persevere. Take consolation in the fact that many Balinese drummers spend the better part of their training perfecting Baris patterns.

We have now described what most of the instruments in the gamelan are doing while the Baris melody is in its stable state. The only exceptions have been the *suling* which essentially follows the ugal melody, and the *cengceng*, which play at the same rate as the drums and reyong, lining every subdivision of the beat with a sparkling metallic edge. The cengceng part can be sung *ch-k- ch-k-ch-k-ch-k* using a breathy and dry quality of voice.

Interaction With the Dance

All of the ways in which the music and dance move between stable and active states involve communication originating with the dancer and are interpreted sonically by the lead kendang. Some dance movements like the *seledet* (a quick flicking of the eyes to the extreme left or right and then back to center) are answered by the drums and cengceng alone. In other more developed angsel, the whole gamelan gets into the act.

With preparatory gestures the dancer signals what he is about to do and the lead drummer, fluent in the language of the dance, knows precisely how and when to react to it. It is the prerogative of the dancer to initialize such movements as he sees fit, but his precise choice is limited by the structure of the music. That is, he must always begin and end the angsel at places predetermined in relation to the gongan structure. This means that the dancer must be as conversant with the music as the lead drummer is with the dance.

The seledet and other small movements of the head and/or upper body alone are echoed instantaneously by a crisp *pak* stroke or two from the kendang. These can occur at a few different places within the cycle; most often they fall immediately after the 7th beat. Since the rest of the gamelan is not involved, the lead drummer need only abandon his normal part for a moment to deliver the required accent and then resume it as before at the next repetition of the melody.

The full angsel are of two types: *bawak* (short) and *lantang* (long). In the former (heard on track 2 at :048, :059, and many other moments), the dancer dramatically lifts his bearing about halfway through the cycle. The

lead kendang reacts just before gong with a series of right hand accents—
dug du'dug!—that shatter the hushed and tense poise of the ensemble. Led
by the ugal, the rest of the players explode into action at the arrival of gong,
playing their parts at peak intensity. The dancer lunges and pivots and, for
a few exhilarating seconds he, the drummers and the ensemble are coordinated in a terrible rush of energy.

Then, before we can even expel our breath, the dancer finds his footing
and the reyong, gangsa, kendang and cengceng come to an abrupt halt.
There are a few beats of repose as the core melody and gongs are revealed,
an inexorable current flowing beneath the vicissitudes of the dance. A final,
biting *kap-pak* from the drummers' interlocking left hand strokes puts an
emphatic period on the sentence. At gong the rest of the gamelan enters as
before, ready to renew the process at the whim of the dancer a few cycles
hence. The full *angsel bawak* process is diagrammed below, showing the
interaction of the dancer and musicians in relation to the kempli beat. The
entire process takes two full cycles.

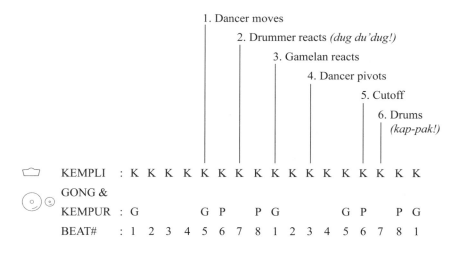

1. Dancer moves
2. Drummer reacts *(dug du'dug!)*
3. Gamelan reacts
4. Dancer pivots
5. Cutoff
6. Drums *(kap-pak!)*

	KEMPLI	: K K K K K K K K K K K K K K K K K
	GONG &	
	KEMPUR	: G G P P G G P P G
	BEAT#	: 1 2 3 4 5 6 7 8 1 2 3 4 5 6 7 8 1

The *angsel lantang* (at 2:04 and 3:40 on track 2), as the name implies, is
longer and also more complex than the angsel bawak. It is initiated when
the dancer assumes a curious half-stooped position, as though preparing to
spring upwards, immediately after an angsel bawak. The kendang answer
with a special cue and at gong the gamelan responds with a crashing accent,

just as it did before. Except that this time the core melody changes, caus-
ing the gangsa to leap into the higher registers and the kotekan to change
too. Only the gilak form outlined by the gongs and kempli is constant. This
dynamic and unexpected disruption is the climax of the performance. For
several cycles the dancer and the gamelan swoop and soar through alternating passages of loud and soft, release and tension, movement and restraint.
At last the dancer concludes the angsel by initiating another angsel bawak.
As the gamelan follows, the melody returns to its former position and the
music resumes as before.

Although it is true that the ordering of the angsel is at the dancer's discre-
tion, in practice this turns out to be not entirely the case. Most dancers and
gamelan that work together regularly establish a more or less set choreography that varies but little from performance to performance. This usually
consists of a relatively static opening that builds to several angsel bawak
and one angsel lantang. Up to this point, the dancer has used only a part of
the stage. During the next section, movement is much freer as the dancer
traces the perimeter of the space, in the process interpolating many angsel
bawak. The cue for the second angsel lantang is also the cue for the immi-
nent ending. Following the angsel, the lead kendang gives a signal which
communicates instructions for the final repetition of the cycle, which is in
a slower, more cadential tempo.

What has been explicated above is only the first of the three large sections in a Baris performance. The second one, which follows immediately,
is called the *bapang*. It has a different structure and is itself divided into
three parts which share a single core melody but are distinguished from
each other by their tempi: fast, slow, fast. The final part of Baris returns to
the gilak.

CHAPTER SIX

Ensembles and Repertoire

Bali has developed and nourished an astonishing variety of musical ensembles—a kaleidoscope of sound and rhythm all the more remarkable because of the island's tiny size. There are more than two dozen distinct species of *gamelan*, each with an established tradition, repertoire, and social or religious context. Some, like the *gamelan gong kebyar*, are to be found by the hundreds all over the island, from the most isolated mountain hamlets to the crowded neighborhoods of Denpasar. Some are less common but thrive nevertheless, like the intimate chamber music of the shadow play's *gamelan gender wayang*. Others are strange, often sacred anomalies found in only a few villages or temples, particularly in the lush eastern and northeastern hills.

It is almost sufficient to point to the creative vigor and experimental predilections of the Balinese as an explanation for this diversity. Certainly no other place in the world, large or small, has proportionately as much or as many kinds of music in it as Bali does, and this happy state of affairs can only be attributed to the efforts of the Balinese. But other more concrete factors have always been present to provide a context for such elusive variables as artistic temperament to assert themselves. One of those crucial elements is the topography of the island. Bali is sliced north/south by a network of deep ravines that, until the modern era, severely limited interaction between denizens of even closely situated villages. As a result, many styles of music developed in relative isolation from one another.

Economics and patronage have played important roles, too. In the past, some gamelan found nurturance exclusively in the courts, either because they were massive and hence beyond the financial reach of the villages, or else because their esthetic qualities were too refined to earn a meaningful place in the lives of any but the leisure class. Still, the musicians employed in the courts were common folk, and the musical education they received at work was put to good use at home supplementing the established grass-roots traditions. Aristocratic styles of music frequently took hold outside the palace walls, often transformed and adapted for less ostentatious bamboo instruments. Many kinds of bamboo ensembles also have their own histories, and plenty of enthusiasts in communities all over Bali. But even in such villages, there has never been an adequate substitute for the powerful sound and aura of a bronze gamelan, in particular the large gongs at the heart of them. Few communities would deign to entertain visiting deities without one.

Repertoire in Balinese music was entirely dependent on ensemble and context until the 20th century. Every piece of music was associated with a specific type of gamelan and intended for a rigidly prescribed occasion. Sacred music was for use only in the temples and music for entertainment was kept out in no uncertain terms. To have suggested otherwise would have been tantamount to heresy. Today these restrictions have been relaxed somewhat and many sacred compositions have found their way into secular life, often in transformation form and adapted for recreational gamelan (although this process does not go in the reverse direction). This does not necessarily lessen the music's ritual power, though, because when such pieces are played in the sanctum sanctorum an entirely different set of standards continues to apply—one wholly indifferent to life outside the temple.

One could fill volumes with just the titles for all the different pieces of music in the repertoires of Balinese ensembles, notwithstanding the repetition and confusion engendered when, as often happens, the same name is used for two unrelated compositions. Conversely, neighboring villages sometimes use different names for one and the same piece! Equally confusing but far more demanding of scrutiny is the matter of regional variation.

Rarely is a single piece of music played precisely the same way by any two groups. It may only be on the level of minute detail, such as a turn in a *kotekan* rhythm or the ordering of a sequence of *angsel*, or it may be some more substantial component of the music—but these differences are justly treasured by musicians. "This is how we play it in our village!" is a frequently heard boast. Sadly, these strains of individuality are today under siege. It is often difficult for regional styles to hold their own against the democratizing effects of mass media and centralized education in a fast-shrinking world. Negara and Amlapura, at opposite ends of the island, are no longer as far away from each other as they once were.

Fortunately, the family of ensembles has so far proved mostly impervious to the forces conspiring against stylistic diversity. *Kebyar* threatened to eclipse some of its ancestors for a time, but the danger seems to have passed. Some ensembles have outlived their functional role in Balinese life, but academics and preservationists are certain to keep them alive for the foreseeable future. In the meantime the whole world of Balinese music is there to be heard by adventurous music lovers. Most of it is readily accessible; hearing certain kinds may take a little advance planning. All of it is well worth the effort. And if the opportunity to hear a live performance cannot be arranged, almost everything is available on recordings.

The survey of gamelan undertaken in the following pages is far from exhaustive. It covers the most important styles and a few more esoteric ones, providing information about the tuning, instruments, traditional context, and any noteworthy musical idiosyncrasies. There is also mention of which villages host the most prominent representatives of the genre. In this regard it should be noted that the KOKAR/SMKI and ISI conservatories own, between them, at least one set of instruments for every type of gamelan, but these are mainly for study purposes and as such are not classified here along with the indigenous groups. We begin with the bronze ensembles, move on to gamelan in which bamboo is the primary sound-producing material, and introduce some sacred ensembles and miscellany. The chapter concludes with an overview of Balinese vocal music genres.

Gamelan gong kebyar, fronted by the *trompong*, playing a modernized *lelambatan* melody.

PART I: BRONZE GAMELAN ENSEMBLES

Gamelan Gong Kebyar

Throughout this book gamelan gong kebyar has been the "default" ensemble for discussing musical instruments and technicalities because it is the orchestra that visitors are most likely to encounter in a formal performance setting, and the kind of gamelan that most Balinese are likely to know something about. There are many who bemoan kebyar's near-hegemony, but such certainly is the reality. If kebyar's resources have indeed proved to be a fertile ground for musical development, perhaps that can be attributed to its birth as a secular and populist ensemble, independent of ritual constraints and the behests of nobility. *Gong kebyar* has absorbed and processed all of the old styles on which it is directly based, filched a bit of material from ensembles with which it has only a tangential relationship, and above all synthesized all of this to produce a dazzling, ultra-modern repertoire of its own. It is, as ethnologist Miguel Covarrubias wrote, "the modern concert orchestra par excellence."[1]

---

1   Covarrubias, Miguel, *Island of Bali*, Alfred A. Knopf, New York, 1937.

Kebyar is usually translated as "to burst open," like a flower in sudden bloom, or "to flare up," like a match. The word itself, heavily stressed on the second syllable and with a pronounced roll on the "r," is an onomatopoetic simulation of the ensemble's signature sound: an explosive, throbbing unison attack. The instruments are tuned to a five-tone *pélog* mode with a moderately fast paired tuning that emphasizes their rich resonance. A full battery of tuned bronze metallophones, an assortment of gongs, *cengceng*, *suling* and large *kendang* all conspire to create a sound of riveting power.

The music of the gamelan gong kebyar exploits the particular capabilities of the instruments in the ensemble. The 10-key range of the 4 *pemadé*, 4 *kantilan* and the *ugal* make broad and adventurous melodies possible. The *reyong*, composed of twelve small gongs, and played by four musicians, is used in a number of ways which make a salient contribution to the music. Sometimes it bursts free from the texture to play dazzling "solos" (quartets, actually, since there are four musicians involved) on its own. Another characteristic reyong sound is *ocak-ocakan*, a combination of 8 tones sounded together in a brassy chord and combined with the kendang and cengceng. The gongs are also played on the lower rim, which results in a sound similar to that of the cengceng. And of course it also plays along melodically, fitting in with the rest of the ensemble in a more conventional manner.

At the time of its inception, kebyar music was largely a hodgepodge of borrowed material and pastiches clothed in musical modernisms. It began to accumulate its own repertoire after the 1920s, when a dancer from Tabanan village named Maria (Mah-ree-yhe) took the Balinese scene by storm. His creations interpreted the capricious nature of the new music with free form choreographies that featured intricate movements of the upper body and a wide range of facial expressions. The Kebyar Duduk, or sitting kebyar, and Kebyar Trompong, in which the dancer performs upon the trompong amid great histrionics, swept the island, and Maria was instantly in demand everywhere as a teacher of the new style.

Maria's creations helped to coin an entire genre known as *tari lepas*— free dances. Free in this context refers not to the choreography, as most tari lepas music and dance are meticulously planned down to the last angsel, but rather to the brevity of the performance and its independence from any larger theatrical form. Kebyar Duduk, Kebyar Trompong, and dozens of others that subsequently joined the repertoire now form the substance of an evening's kebyar performance, augmented with some more classical dances—Baris, for example, and perhaps even Legong. Other important tari lepas include Oleg Tambulilingan (created by Maria in 1951 for the Peliatan gamelan's world tour), which portrays two bumblebees in courtship, and the powerful Taruna Jaya (Victorious Youth) from North Bali, a long and demanding dance of great subtlety and beauty that has become a true Balinese classic. Taruna Jaya and the related dances Kebyar Legong and Taruna Gandrung, are virtuoso efforts for both musicians and dancers and are considered to be the quintessential kebyar-style pieces. One reliable test of a drummer's mettle is the ease with which he can negotiate performances of them.

Rounding out tari lepas performances are the new instrumental compositions, the established medium for musical experimentation. From the early days such pieces featured, among other revolutionary musical devices, the occasional abandonment of *gongan* as a unifying principle, the substitution of free rhythm for steady pulse, abrupt stops and starts, and musical forms based around a series of melodic snippets rather than a substantial main movement. Melodies of breadth and scope gave way to a musical language that aimed for virtuosity, speed and special effects. The novelty could not last, of course, but the best musicians were ultimately able to transcend the limits of music based on such superficial notions to create works of elegance and integrity.

The more or less standard form for kebyar instrumental compositions (*kreasi baru*, as they are usually called) that emerged during the middle of the century consists of five sections separated by transition passages. There are generally two ways to begin a piece. One is the kebyar proper—a jagged, irregular and forceful melody played in perfect unison by the entire ensemble. Only the *kempli* is silent, as no regular beat is intended. The amount of practice needed to perfect the coordination of such unstable rhythms is evident, and the effect in performance is electric. Another kind of opening is the *gineman*—a series of short phrases separated by pauses. Each of the phrases may involve a different combination of instruments, but the predominant sound is that of little bursts of kotekan and melody played by the *gangsa, calung* and *jegogan*. Three internal sections, connected to each other by freely composed links, succeed to the opening. They showcase, in any order, interlocking rhythmic variations for the drums, gangsa, and the reyong. A finale for the whole gamelan closes the piece in a boisterous and flamboyant fashion.

Most kreasi baru have shown themselves to be pretty ephemeral; only some pieces have demonstrated staying power. The reason for this is not necessarily connected to any notions of quality, rather it is a function of the great quantity of compositions that have appeared. Groups tiring of a given piece simply request new ones from their resident director or from an outside composer. Plus, yearly festivals mandate new work on a regular basis, which discourages reuse of older music. But a few kreasi baru, even if not played regularly anymore, have attained "classic" status: Gambang Suling, composed in the 1960s and based partly on a tuneful Javanese melody of the period, is one such piece. Another is Kosalia Arini, popularized on the radio in the 1970s. Kapi Raja and Jaya Semara are two nearly identical kebyar-style compositions that have also proven very durable; the latter can be heard on the book CD, track 3.

The short history of kebyar has already borne witness to the rise and fall of a pantheon of musical giants. In the beginning the Singaraja area monopolized the scene with famous groups in the neighboring villages of Jagaraga and Sawan. The former was the birthplace of the influential drummer and teacher Gdé Manik. These villages (and many others in North Bali) still have active gamelan associations, but their island-wide fame has diminished. From the 30s to the 60s the crown was passed between a number of villages around Denpasar—Belaluan, Sadmertha, and Sibang, to name a few—and the village of Peliatan some 20-odd kilometers to the north. Pressure to innovate was fierce in those days, and inter-group competition was cutthroat. Tales of spies sent to observe rival groups' rehearsals and enormous fees paid to secure exclusive rights to a teacher for a new piece (plans often frustrated by sabotage and shady dealing) illustrate the ruthless zeal with which the new music was propagated.

Two groups that emerged in the 1960s are still very famous among the older generations today, although they are more or less dormant unless fulfilling obligations to perform sacred music in the temple or playing for some other special occasion. These are in the villages of Geladag, south of Denpasar, and Pindha, near Blahbatuh in Gianyar district. Each is situated in an area that has been musically fertile since long before the advent of kebyar. Mention of either group will kindle flames of near-nationalistic fervor in the eyes of Balinese who live anywhere around either of those places. Both maintain expansive repertoires of *lelambatan* for use in the temple as well as an array of modern dance and music pieces, which in many cases were given their first and definitive performances by these groups. To hear the best of kebyar while in Bali, it is well worth inquiring as to whether or not either the Pindha or Geladag group is engaged for a temple or recreational performance. Recordings of these ensembles are still in circulation, hence the particular depth and mastery of their players remain a model of both technical brilliance and unselfconscious soul. They represent the height of kebyar's 20th century florescence.

No gamelan in the past half century (save for the conservatory groups) has achieved enough fame to challenge the supremacy of Pindha and Geladag. One close contender emerged in the 1970s in the village of Perean, Tabanan district. A recording of their ensemble from that period displays the absolute summit of gamelan speed and virtuosity: kotekan played at a rate of 200 beats per minute. At four subdivisions per beat that breaks down to 800 notes per minute, or an average of 400 notes each for *polos* and *sangsih* parts, which in turn translates to almost 7 notes per player per second! Can one conceive of 25 people doing *anything* together that fast? All of this was executed with crystalline clarity and accompanied, one might surmise, by facial expressions of utter nonchalance and boredom during performance. Regrettably, Perean's group disbanded soon after those recordings were made. Some of the musicians and their families subsequently transmigrated to Sumatra on an Indonesian government resettlement and land development program. In the spring of 1989, however, a revival organized by some of those who remained behind led to some very strong comeback performances.

In the 1980s the kebyar scene was dominated by music made at the conservatories, and by the groups that participated in the yearly Festival Gong. For the latter, each spring two different groups—one male and one female—from each of Bali's 8 *kabupaten* (plus a 9th district, Denpasar city) are chosen to represent their area with a number of standard and newly created works. The rotation ensures that over a period of years as many villages as possible participate and, for better or worse, keeps the public eye from focusing on any particular one for too long. The competing groups are judged each June by an island-wide panel of experts and winners are chosen.

Mention should be made of some prominent individuals who shaped the history of kebyar in the 20th century. By far the single most revered, older musician in all of Balinese music today is I Wayan Beratha (b. 1924), whose father Madé Regog was the head of the gamelan from Belaluan in the 1930s. Beratha's influence as a drummer and composer is still felt everywhere. He was also active as a tuner and gamelan merchant. Other important figures are I Nyoman Rembang of Sesetan, Badung, a noted scholar and music historian; I Wayan Begeg of Pangkung, Tabanan, I Madé Terip of Munduk, Buleleng, and I Wayan Tembres of Blangsinga, Gianyar. One of the most outstanding performers is I Wayan Suweca of Denpasar, whose prowess as a drummer is well-known. Suweca is a lecturer at the conservatory, and his colleagues both in and out of school comprise the finest talents of his generation. (Tembres and Suweca will be profiled in depth in Chapters Eight and Ten, respectively.) There are too many outstanding players in the younger generations to note here individually, but there are enough to guarantee the vitality of gamelan gong kebyar for some time to come.

Gamelan Semar Pegulingan/Gamelan Pelegongan

For Balinese these two closely related ensembles evoke pleasant and ethereal images of a not-too-distant past whose elegant sensibilities have lately been trampled by too much modernism too fast. It is certainly true that there are only a handful of these high-pitched, sweet-sounding gamelan extant now, whereas there were hundreds in the 1930s and '40s. *Semar pegulingan* is a seven-tone pélog ensemble with a repertoire derived from the *gamelan gambuh*. It features a *trompong* on the lead melody part. The elaboration instruments are of but 7 keys each (one octave range), as are the jegogan and calung. No reyong is present. The large gong is supplanted by the *kempur* and the kempli by the bossless *kajar*. The kendang are small too, and there are a variety of tiny, chiming cymbal-like instruments that fill out the orchestra. The music of Semar pegulingan is sensuous and perfumed, with all manner of plaintive melodies and tonal colors resulting from the added dimensions of the full 7-tone scale.

There are only a few 7-tone semar pegulingan groups in Bali with long histories. One is in the village of Kamasan, Klungkung district, and the others are in Denpasar at Banjars Pagan Kelod, Sesetan Kaja, and Tampak Gangsul. Except for in Kamasan, the younger generation has not learned the tradition, which is now carried only by some very old men. In Kamasan the music has been nourished and the ensemble is active, at least at ceremony time. Young people in the village have taken a special interest in the music of late as well. Luckily, the conservatories have been instrumental in promoting awareness of semar pegulingan music, releasing in the early '90s a comprehensive collection of the ensemble's classic repertoire. As a result there are signs of a kind of transplantation to several places where the music did not exist before. Banjar Abiankapas in Denpasar acquired an ensemble, as did *banjar* Mekar Sari of Padang Tegal, near Ubud. Though its survival once seemed dicey, the music of semar pegulingan has found new footing.

The same combination of instruments mentioned above, but restricted to 5-tone pélog and augmented by two gender, are also referred to as semar pegulingan. The gender are of 13, 14 or 15 keys each and are played in octaves with two mallets, which produces a delicate sound that adds a lilting, wistful air to the music. In some compositions, when the trompong is not used, this kind of gamelan is also called *pelegongan* because that particular configuration of instruments is primarily associated with performances of the repertoire of *legong keraton* dances. This is the gamelan that reigned during the colonial period and charmed Colin McPhee into devoting himself so assiduously to Balinese music. Pelegongan music is by turns majestic and moving, playful and winsome, and without any of the aggressive tendencies of kebyar. For gamelan connoisseurs, it is the classiest and wittiest music on the island.

Legong keraton (or simply legong) is not a single dance, as it is often misunderstood to be, but in fact a whole genre of choreographies, each with its own musical accompaniment. The Lasem story is the most popular. It portrays an old Javanese tale of the kidnapping of a princess and her abductor's confrontation by a bird of ill omen while on the way to do battle for his honor. Also an important part of the pelegongan repertoire is the Calonarang play, a 16th century tale of witchcraft and terror in a Balinese village which features the beloved dragon-protector Barong and the despised witch Rangda. The Calonarang music for the *sisya*, or dance of the witch's disciples, is one of the most haunting and beautiful melodies in all of Balinese music. No pelegongan performance would be complete without an instrumental piece or two. Some of these are adapted from the 7-tone semar pegulingan repertoire; others were bequeathed by the patriarch of pelegongan music, I Lotring, or by one of the many other composers active during his era. Lotring's music is represented on track 5 of the book CD by the imaginative composition Solo.

There are wonderful pelegongan/semar pegulingan ensembles to be heard in the villages of Tista, near Kerambitan, Binoh, northwest of Denpasar, Teges Kanginan, just east of Peliatan, and Ketewel, near Sukawati. The legong tradition in Ketewel is notable for its close connections to the history of the form. The village possesses a unique set of eight sacred female masks that are used in performances of a progenitor of the modern legong, the *legong bidedari*. Although the account is unsubstantiated, this dance is said to have originated in the visions of a priest who lived in Ketewel near the end of the 19th century. Bidedari are angels; the priest reported witnessing a beautiful dance by two angels in heaven while meditating. Choreographies were later devised, on the instructions of the priest, to reproduce what he had seen. The young dancers were required to perform with the masks so that the spirits of the angels might enter them. Later, in the early part of this century, the *raja* of nearby Sukawati village oversaw the adaptation and transformation of the legong bidedari choreographies into what evolved as the modern legong. The sacred masks, however, are still danced at important ceremonies in Ketewel. In Peliatan village the excellent Tirtha Sari group gives a weekly performance with some elegant and authentic pieces, as well as others that have been thoroughly kebyar-ized. Important personages in the pelegongan world include I Wayan Sinti and his father I Ketut Sadia of Binoh (Sinti is now retired from the KOKAR/SMKI conservatory). Three elder statesmen—I Madé Grindem of the Teges group, Anak Agung Gdé Raka of Saba village, and I Madé Lebah of Peliatan—were particularly celebrated and revered in their day. Lebah's career stretched back to 1931, when he performed with the group from Peliatan in Paris and romanced both the Parisian public and the group's legong dancers—one of whom he later married—with his agile drumming. Throughout the '30s Lebah was Colin McPhee's guide, chauffeur, teacher, and all around right-hand man. Up to his death in late 1996 he continued to teach gamelan from time to time.

Gamelan Gender Wayang

Many visitors to Bali hear their first Balinese music played on a pair or quartet of *gender wayang*, placed off to the side in the hotel lobby. Being relegated to background accompaniment is too often the status quo for this elite chamber gamelan. But its players, over the generations, have slyly exacted their revenge by concocting the most complex, technically difficult, and respected music on the island.

Four ten-key, *slendro*-tuned gender make up the complete ensemble, although in some specialized contexts drums and gongs are added. Two of the gender are tuned in a medium register and two an octave higher. It is perfectly acceptable for only the larger pair to be used, however, since all of the musical parts are present with *two* players. Each musician uses two mallets to play independent left and right hand parts. Generally the players' right hands play kotekan while the left hands support this with melody, but there are all sorts of exceptions to this. Gender wayang music can feature two different, simultaneous kotekan, *or* even a low-register kotekan underpinning a high, slow-moving melody. The variety of textures and nuances cultivated in the performance of the music is tremendous.

Gender is most often heard at *wayang kulit* (shadow play) performances, but it is also traditionally used to provide instrumental music for tooth filing ceremonies and, strangely enough, at cremations, where its tones are usually lost in the roar of the crowd. But the ensemble's natural environment is behind the flickering images of the Mahabharata epic stories played out on the shadow play screen, matching every detail of the puppeteer's performance with an elaborate musical response.

Shadow plays are preceded by one or more of the many dazzling free instrumental compositions from the ensemble's repertoire. Famous ones include Sekar Gendot, Sekar Sungsang, and Merak Ngelo. Then a long overture, the Pemungkah, accompanies the *dalang*, or puppeteer, as he carefully removes all of the puppets from the wooden box in which they are kept, exposes them to the world of the screen, and then replaces all but the ones to be used for that performance. Next he introduces the *kayornan*, or tree-of-life puppet, intones a series of evocative verses, and the play begins. For the duration of the performance the gender players provide music for all of the dalang's songs, for love scenes and scenes of enchantment or despair, for changes of story locale, and for the plentiful battles that always make up the play's climactic moments.

Balinese musicians who do not play gender wayang hold their counterparts who do in high regard, such is the reputation of the music's difficulty. The gender players themselves are more often than not fanatically dedicated to it. When two such musicians from different regions meet, and if there is a set of gender around, there is bound to be much discussion of stylistic differences and the details of performing particular pieces. Regional variation in gender wayang compositions is the most drastic of all Balinese gamelan, perhaps because the intimate size of the ensemble has always made it feasible for individual musicians to assert themselves and make changes in the inherited repertoire that have distinct and personalized characteristics.

The inseparable arts of puppetry and gender wayang have a long history of cultivation in Sukawati village. In 2006 the gender wayang world lost a reigning and universally revered king, I Wayan Loceng of Sukawati. A scholarly mind and dedicated teacher, Loceng was conversant in all aspects of puppetry, including the mythology and linguistics behind it, as well as being a master of the music. It is unlikely another renaissance man of Loceng's caliber will appear any time soon, but there are many excellent performers of this music. Loceng's disciples in Sukawati such as Ketut Buda Astra strongly carry on for him. Gusti Nyoman Darta of Pengosekan is one of the few to compose new music for the ensemble. Wayan Wija, a popular dalang from Sukawati, developed the *wayang tantri*, using stories from the Tantri series. These tales are roughly analogous to "Aesop's Fables," with their sylvan setting and animal characters. For this he devised an entirely original set of puppets and a new instrumental combination which uses pélog-tuned gender playing in gender wayang style, drums, and gongs.

Other proponents of gender wayang are no less gifted. Musician, dancer, and puppeteer I Nyoman Sumandhi of the KOKAR/SMKI conservatory is originally from Tunjuk village in Tabanan, where he learned his art from his father Rajeg. In Denpasar and environs the children of I Wayan Konolan are much in demand as performers of this style. There are gender wayang styles in North Bali at, among other places, Munduk and Tejakula, in Karangasem at Padangkertha, at Teges village near Peliatan, and in private homes around Bali where the music is studied for the satisfying challenge it provides. Embombuan, a composition from Padangkertha, is heard on track 6 of the CD.

Gamelan Angklung

At temple festivals, the exuberance of the 4-tone *gamelan angklung*'s melodies ring out in bold contrast to the solemn and grave lelambatan compositions often heard playing simultaneously right across the courtyard. While to many outsiders the slendro-derived tuning of the gamelan produces a mood of playfulness and charm, to the Balinese it is sentimental, bittersweet, and an indispensable component of the atmosphere at any meaningful ceremony.

A modern Balinese gamelan angklung comprises 8-12 4-keyed metallophones used for melody or kotekan, a reyong of 8 gongs, 2 jegogan, a small kempur, 2 tiny drums, cengceng, suling and a kind of kempli called *tawatawa*. The word "angklung" originally referred to a bamboo rattle which produces but one tone when shaken. Ensembles of these, tuned to a scale and shaken in alternation to create melodies, are still common in West Java. In Bali they used to be played in conjunction with the bronze instruments,[2] but today they are rarely seen, although people often lament their demise nostalgically.

There is a large repertoire of ancient compositions for gamelan angklung. It is full of whimsical pieces with names like Goak Maling Taloh (Crow Steals Eggs) and Katak Nongkek (Croaking Frog), Capung Manjus (Bathing Dragonfly), and many others attaining significant musical breadth. The final melody of Cerucuk Punyah (Drunken Cerucuk Bird) as played by musicians from Mas, is on the CD, track 7. Having only 4 keys per instrument would seem a limitation, and certainly no one would claim that gamelan angklung has as great an expressive range as any of the larger bronze ensembles. Yet as a rule angklung music is full of supple melodies and inventive kotekan, which often breathe and flow in quite unexpected directions. A number of angklung around the island, particularly in the north, use the full 5-tone slendro scale for the additional possibilities it provides, with the size of the instruments expanded accordingly, sometimes up to as many as seven keys. This serves to drastically reduce the constraints imposed by the 4-tone version, substantially altering the personality of the resultant music in the process.

There may be more sets of gamelan angklung in Bali than there are gamelan gong kebyar. Most villages have at least one or two. The village of Mas alone had, at one point, seven; their players have a tough time with schedul-

---

2 Colin McPhee reintroduced them in Sayan village in 1938, when he bought a *gamelan angklung* for the village children. (Sec Chapter One epigraph.)

ing, because a local temple festival lasts only a few days! But the temple is not the only place to hear angklung. Because of the instruments' portability, they are often strung up on bamboo poles and carried in processions. Some tari lepas and kreasi baru have been adapted for the ensemble, thus creating the secular subgenre of *angklung kebyar*. One of the most famous traditional gamelan angklung can be found in the village of Sidan, on the road between Gianyar and Bangli. Another is in Kerambitan village, Tabanan district.

Gamelan Gong Gdé/Gamelan Gong

The enormous *gong gdé* (great gong) ensemble, ancestral progenitor of gong kebyar and indispensable arm of Bali's bygone royal courts, is a splendid anachronism today. Every facet of gong gdé music—the slow, regal tempi, the bald simplicity of the melodic style, the crushing weight of the bronze keys and the mallets used to strike them—exudes majesty, pomp and ceremony mighty enough to call the Gods to attention.

More is better in gong gdé. Extra calung and jegogan, two trompong, gigantic drums and gongs, and pair after pair of large cengceng and *saron*-style gangsa make up the ensemble, which takes up to 50 people to play. Only the reyong is small, with but four gongs. The tunings are dramatic and deep, employing a 5-tone pélog. The gong gdé's repertoire of lelambatan and dance music is vast—although one can only imagine how many more pieces there were at one time, when this orchestra's presence was requisite in the courts.

Up until the establishment of the colonial administration and the gradual decline of the court-village hierarchies in Bali, the gamelan gong gdé was one of the foremost symbols of the courts' opulence. No village could have ever afforded to maintain an orchestra of that size. But by the late 19th century many villages were casting scaled-down versions of the gong gdé that could approximate the sound of the original without unduly straining municipal and temple budgets. This ensemble, rarely heard today, became known simply as the gamelan gong.

History has shown that the gamelan gong served some important functions at the time. It helped to disseminate the music of the royal court in the villages, and it also exposed that music to the influence of other gamelan styles. In gamelan gong music, for instance, lelambatan melodies were elaborated with simple kotekan on the gangsa for the first time, whereas in gong gdé this is limited to the tiny reyong used. Gamelan gong served as a kind of transitional phase before the advent of gamelan gong kebyar, which quickly proved up to subsuming all of its functions. By the time of Indonesian independence most gamelan gong had been melted down and recast as the streamlined kebyar. There are some left; one is in Demulih village, near Bangli. This is the ensemble playing on track 8 of the CD.

With the exception of an ensemble that is kept in Denpasar, the few original gong gdé still played in Bali are scattered around Bangli district. There is one in the village of Sulahaan which is reputed to have been bequeathed by the king of Bangli when the court disbanded. Another is kept in the temple overlooking Lake Batur, where it plays regularly for festivals. The powerful tolling of the gong gdé during a moonlit ceremony is a stirring musical reminder of a Bali that is now part of the past.

PART II: BAMBOO GAMELAN ENSEMBLES

Tingklik and Gamelan Joged Bumbung

The Balinese gamelan that use bamboo tubes or slats rather than bronze slabs for keys are the true folk music of Bali, in the sense that they were never courtly arts. This in no way implies, however, that the music made on them is in any way simpler or less rigorous in construction. It is only that the occasions on which they are played are more often impromptu and meant mostly to be for fun and diversion. Bamboo music is very much on an earthly plane, refreshingly free of any pretenses to sublimity.

Tingklik is the most common name for a bamboo instrument made of a series of tubes tuned to a scale and strung up in ascending order in a simple frame. Almost any Balinese with a little acquired expertise could easily construct one by just using materials found growing in his or her backyard; doubtless the origin of the tingklik traces to some leisurely tinkerers and their serendipitous experimentations in at-home bamboo laboratories. Long before anyone had the idea of combining groups of such instruments into ensembles, people were improvising melodies on them in their spare time. From these modest beginnings, a world of music grew.

Most tingklik are tuned to a slendro scale and played with two spindly, rubber-tipped mallets. Bamboo has virtually no sustaining resonance on its own and emits a very dry sound when struck, so the tubes need not be damped between tones like bronze keys. This makes tingklik easier to play than gender, while requiring more force to make the tubes sound. Coordination between left and right hands is still a challenge. Pairs of tingklik play melody and kotekan in a kind of gender wayang style when heard, as they often are, in hotels and restaurants. The sweet and unobtrusive charm of their music, often augmented with a melodious suling or two, has a great appeal for many visitors.

A group of four or more tingklik with added flutes, drums and an ersatz gong made by hanging an enormous bamboo key (metal is sometimes used) over a resonator is called *gamelan joged bumbung*, or just *gamelan joged* for short. It is primarily used as an accompaniment for the *joged* dance, wherein a single girl dancer taunts male members of the audience into joining her in a flirtatious and often hilarious improvised duet. The men are not necessarily trained dancers, but they are expected to sink or swim. This creates a little embarrassment sometimes, but more often than not just gales of good-natured laughter.

The origins of gamelan joged melodies are usually a mystery, even to the musicians who play them. Some come from popular songs; others have been composed by the players themselves. For tingklik duets and quartets some pieces have been appropriated directly from gamelan gender wayang. Most have anonymous origins, having emerged somewhere along the path of the music's development.

Locating good joged ensembles is difficult, as they seem to form and disband as quickly as their instruments can be constructed or disassembled. There are famous ones near the city of Gianyar and in Sanur that are often in demand to provide an evening's entertainment. Banjar Kalah, Peliatan, has a gamelan joged that is mostly dormant but pops up unexpectedly for revivals. Joged groups are frequently engaged by families undertaking a private ceremony that wish to repay the members of their village for the substantial amount of community labor that is always donated on such occasions.

In northern and western Bali, they take their gamelan joged very seriously. In fact western Bali is the only part of the island that perhaps cares a bit more for bamboo music than it does for bronze. Expanded ensembles made from larger and more richly sonorous bamboo play music for joged dancers, pieces transplanted from the kebyar repertoire, and indigenous instrumental works with phenomenal brilliance and clarity. This style of joged can be heard in Jembrana at Tegalcangkering, in Tabanan at Luwus, and in Buleleng at Sangsit. The Tegalcangkering group plays an excerpt from one of their most kebyar-ized pieces on track 9.

Gamelan Jegog

Bamboo grown in west Bali reaches monstrous proportions the likes of which are not known elsewhere on the island. This quirk of nature has been exploited by local musicians with the creation of the *gamelan jegog*, so named for the remarkable jegogan that is the sonic core of the ensemble. Individual tubes on these may stretch to an incredible 3 meters in length, with circumferences of 60–65 centimeters.[3] They are so unwieldy that a pair of musicians must sit on top of the frame of the instrument in order to play it. It requires quite a pounding with thick rubber beaters to coax music out of them, but what finally emerges is a sound so powerful that it seems to enter the body through the stomach rather than the ears.

Jegog is tuned to an unusual and haunting 4-tone scale which, it is speculated, was derived from tones 2, 3, 5, and 7 of the full 7-tone pélog (see Chapter Three). All of the instruments have 8 tubes. On the jegogan and the two calung tuned an octave above them, the 4 right-hand tubes duplicate the tones of those on the left, enabling the players to play rolling melodies by alternating left and right hand strokes between notes of the same pitch. The upper register instruments play melodies and kotekan, including a special style of kotekan called *slanketan*, in which individual players negotiate parts of both polos and sangsih at once. Melodic and rhythmic cycles are arranged into episodic compositions, the lengths of which can be prolonged or foreshortened simply by repeating any of the sections more or fewer times.

Great crowds gather when two, three or more *jegog* groups assemble in an open field of an evening to *mabarung*—play competition style. At first, the idea is to scrutinize the quality of the instruments' sound, the musical content and the technical skill of the players. The opening strains of each

---

3   This seems particularly surreal when one recalls that botanically speaking, bamboo is actually just a species of grass.

gamelan's music are carefully examined for these qualities. As the evening progresses, the groups begin to play simultaneously in a cacophony of short, driving ostinato patterns. The focus then shifts to determining who can play louder, harder and for as long as possible without stopping or losing their place in the melody. Shirts soak through with sweat and fingers get ravaged by blisters as musicians push themselves to the absolute limits of their physical abilities in pursuit of such distinctions. Around 2 a.m., after a trial by a jury of peers, the exhausted players finally disperse.

Jegog is extremely popular in Jembrana and lately has spread to Denpasar and Ubud too. In Jembrana any single village may have 5 or 6 active groups. The villages of Tegalcangkering and Sangkaragung are among the best known. A walk down the main street of either of these towns at night is bound to lead to a lively rehearsal hall or two that is filled with the colorfully painted jegog instruments and a group of musicians playing them with abandon. It is worth a trip to this little-visited part of Bali just to hear their ecstatic music in its original setting.

Gamelan Gandrung

The *gandrung* ensemble, once popular as an accompaniment to a joged-like dance of the same name, bears mention even though it is nearly extinct. The 5-tone pélog-tuned instruments are constructed of wooden slats suspended over bamboo resonators much in the manner of gender, and are played in octaves with a mallet in each hand. The ensemble also includes the usual complement of kendang and other percussion. The gandrung style of playing kotekan is famous among Balinese musicians for being second in complexity only to that of gender wayang. Even though the music is rarely heard today, its influence is felt in many kebyar pieces.

During the colonial period gandrung ensembles proliferated. Today the only extant gandrung groups are in Ketapian Kelod, on the outskirts of Denpasar, and in Tegunungan, south of Kemenuh village in Gianyar district. The former achieved some renown during the 1920s, when it was led by Nyoman Kaler, a famous drummer, composer and choreographer. But Kaler's services were much in demand and he did not stay with the group long. In subsequent years the flirtatious gandrung dance, too, fell from esteem in the public's eye. Some time ago, Ketapian's village elders were wise enough to declare the ensemble *keramat*—sacred—thereby ensuring its survival through mandatory usage in temple rituals. This precious ensemble's music is heard on track 10 of the CD.

PART III: SACRED AND RARE ENSEMBLES

Gamelan Selonding

Gamelan selonding (or *selunding*) is one of a group of 7-tone pélog ensembles in Bali distinguished by their ancient origins and extremely sacred connotations. They are among the oldest ensembles on the island, predating the gamelan gambuh. Selonding is associated with the Bali Aga, or so-called pre-Hindu villages scattered about the hills of eastern Bali. Many of the instruments used, and almost all of the compositions played on it are considered to have been bequeathed to the villagers by deities in the mythological past.

These gamelan are used only in specific ritual contexts, and elaborate offerings must be made prior to playing them. The instruments themselves, as well as the compositions played on them, are indispensable components in the successful completion of annual ceremonial rites; by extension they are also considered necessary for maintaining the general spiritual well-being of the village and its members.

Selonding is the only gamelan with keys cast from iron. The keys are strung up over low troughs and played with club-shaped mallets in an unusual two-handed technique. Although the makeup of the gamelan varies from village to village, it is often composed exclusively of these instruments, although a set of cengceng may be added for music that accompanies dance. Selonding melody and figuration has a soft rippling sound quite distinct from the piercing sonority of bronze.

Some well-known selonding ensembles are kept in the eastern villages of Asak, Rungaya, and Tangkas. The village of Tenganan is notable for its 3 selonding ensembles, which are stored in individual sheds lined up north-south along the terraced main street. These are acknowledged to be man-made copies of an original, God-given gamelan, which is never actually used in performance. The ones that may be played are brought out at festival time and set up on raised platforms within sight and reach only of the specially designated performers. The instruments must undergo costly purification rites if their sanctity is degraded by the touch or glance of outsiders.

This last statement requires qualification. After centuries of fiercely guarding selonding's purity Tenganan has relaxed some restrictions. The village instruments are still protected, but recordings have been made and distributed commercially—a previously unthinkable act of disrespect. Copies of the ensembles are now in the possession of the conservatories, and numerous villages and private organizations, where this ancient music can be learned in a secular environment. Composer Nyoman Windha created a major new work for selonding instruments called Bali Aga in the early 1990s. These developments have aroused the protests of some observers, but the liberties taken were granted by the Tenganese themselves, so it would seem that the case must rest there.

Gamelan Gambang

The brittle and austere sound of the 7-tone *gamelan gambang* has long been important at cremations, at temple festivals in East Bali, and at other selected ceremonies. It is allied in function with the gamelan selonding where both are found in the same village, but the *gambang*'s domain is more geographically diverse; it is found in northern and southern Bali as well. That the 4 wooden gambang xylophones used in the ensemble have close relatives of the same name in Javanese gamelan is an indication of the instrument's venerable history.

In Bali each gambang is played with a pair of Y-shaped mallets, the twin tips of which are spaced so as to strike tones an octave apart. With the 4 players' 8 hands in constant motion, a dense and involuted kotekan is generated. As in the gamelan gambuh and other 7-tone ensembles, only five of the seven notes are used in any single composition. In gamelan gambang music, virtually all possible distillations of five-note modes from the original seven are found in the repertoire. For the gamelan gambang at Bebetin village, near Singaraja, the modes are named according to the best-known piece in which they are used. The five-note group used in the important composition Semarandhana, for example, is called "Semarandhana mode" even when it is used in other pieces. Of course, as with all systems of nomenclature in Bali, there is considerable variance from one village to the next.

Completing the gamelan are a pair of 7-key bronze saron-style metallophones that ring out brightly with the core melody. This melody is nearly always stated in the characteristic rhythm of 5 + 3 counts, an uneven division of an ordinary 8-beat phrase that is instantly identifiable to most Balinese musicians as *"gambangan* rhythm." It is often used in *gamelan pelegongan* and kebyar compositions for the distinctive flavor that it adds.

Gambang compositions, because of their continuous staid rhythm, are very difficult to learn. None of the four gambangs' keys are laid out in the same way, and each of the four players' parts is different from the others. Moreover, individual pieces are closely connected to verse forms in classical poetry, and it is said to be a frustrating experience at best to attempt to play the music without having mastered the poems first. Perhaps for this reason gambang is usually attractive to scholarly and literary-minded individuals. Wayan Sinti, one such expert, has researched and reconstructed the use of gamelan gambang to accompany to singing, a practice long assumed to have been lost. Well-known gambang traditions are extant in many villages, among them Sempidi, near Denpasar, and Asak, Karangasem district.

Gamelan Luang/Gamelan Gong Bheri

Two other rare and sacred ensembles merit passing mention. *Gamelan luang*, now found only in Sukawati and Singapadu, Gianyar; Kerambitan, Tabanan; Tangkas, Klungkung, and a few other places, is an archaic, 7-tone relative of the *gamelan gong gdé* that combines a mixture of bronze and bamboo instruments. The instrumentation of each *luang* is unique. The repertoire of compositions includes several pieces that equal lelambatan in their scope. In some villages there are close connections to the gamelan gambang tradition as well. The Kerambitan group, following the lead of the selonding from Tenganan village, issued recordings of "New Compositions for Gamelan Luang," thus letting the cat out of the bag. The syncopated melodic style of gamean luang, called *luangan*, influenced composers of new kebyar music in the 1980s and '90s

Renon, a village near Sanur that is seat of Bali's central government, is the only village that cultivates an unusual ensemble of gongs, drums and cengceng called *gamelan gong bheri*, which is used to accompany an even more unusual dance, the Baris Cina (Chinese Baris). Outwardly, the dance has nothing to do with the country, but the instruments of the gamelan are said to have come centuries ago from a Chinese trading ship that ran aground off the coast nearby. The bossless gongs in the gamelan do in fact resemble Chinese tam-tams, so there may well be some truth to the story.

PART IV: OTHER BALINESE ENSEMBLES

Gamelan Baleganjur/Bebonangan

The 4, 5 or 6-part interlocking rhythms of the giant *cengceng kopyak*, as used in the gamelan gong gdé form the basis for certain genres of Balinese music that thrive on the intensity that those patterns generate. One such ensemble is the *bebonangan* or, as it is popularly called, *baleganjur*, a fixture in virtually all religious processions. It is next to impossible to drive around Bali of an afternoon without encountering at least one of these boisterous marching bands bringing up the rear in a parade of colorfully dressed Balinese.

Gamelan baleganjur is actually just a gong kebyar without metallophones, plus several sets of the cengceng. The gongs are strung up on bamboo poles to facilitate carrying them, and the drummers, playing with mallets, hang their instruments around their necks with a cord. To carry the reyong, some of the gongs are removed from their frame and distributed, one to a player. Polos and sangsih are thus further subdivided into two parts each, which results in a 4-part kotekan. Such an arrangement makes the music especially difficult to coordinate, particularly while walking.

The word bebonangan comes from *bonang*, the Javanese word for the type of small gongs used on the reyong and trompong. Baleganjur means, roughly, 'walking army' in Old Javanese, thus signifying marching music. Driven by an authoritative gilak pattern provided by the gongs and kempli, the cengceng, reyong and kendang engage in a three-way musical dialogue of commanding power. The instrumental groups fade in and out of the texture, meeting occasionally for a series of angsel patterns, only to diverge again, melting into the hypnotic pulsing of the gongs. A more compelling type of marching music has yet to be devised.

Beleganjur is loud, infectious, exciting to play, and a particular favorite with young people in Bali today. Ketut Gdé Asnawa, a composer from Kaliungu Kaja, Denpasar, started a craze in 1986 when he formed a recreational baleganjur group in his banjar. He extended the traditional patterns by elaborating the angsel sequences and introducing more kotekan and drum variations. New, lighter-weight cengceng kopyak were devised, allowing for faster and more complex rhythmic patterning. In the years since, so-called *kreasi baleganjur* groups have appeared literally everywhere, often forming or disbanding on a dime. These changes led to popular competitions in which twenty or more groups assemble and file in parade fashion past seated jurors, who evaluate the contestants on their ensemble skill and even on the theatricality of their presentation, which has become a big part of the fun. Make up, outrageous costumes, and even choreographed stepping routines are routinely tossed into the act, adding a tongue-in-cheek dimension to the festivities.

Cak (Kecak)

Cak (often called *kecak* and also known as the "Monkey Chant") is a theatrical performance that enacts the rescue of princess Sita from the demon-king Rawana by an army of monkeys, an important episode in the Hindu Ramayana epic. For cak, no instrument is used but the human voice. The lead dancers and actors are encircled by a male chorus that portrays the monkeys in sound and movement. There are singing parts distributed amongst the chorus and dancers, but the main purpose of the chorus is to emulate the hordes of attackers with a cloud of percussive vocal effects. The syllable *cak*! (*cha'!*), spat out repetitively by the 100 monkeys through clenched teeth in a set of staccato interlocking rhythms creates a sound that evokes the frightening turbulence of the scene.

The cak rhythms are similar to cengceng kopyak patterns. There are up to seven independent parts, none any more than 4 beats in duration. One strong-lunged member of the chorus is called upon to chant a continuous simulated kempli beat (the syllable *pung* sung in a high-pitched and constricted tone is used) with which the interlocking monkeys align themselves. Dancers playing the part of Rawana or the monkey general Hanuman prance about, exhorting or taunting the army to intensify or restrain their chanting with guttural sounds ranging from bursts of controlled rage to uninhibited whoops. At times the chorus breaks from its cak patterns to interject with demonic hisses and yells, or, depending on the dramatic situation, subdued and pious singing.

A *cak* in Teges, created by the Javanese choreographer Sardono.

Cak is and always has been a tourist performance. Walter Spies, the renowned artist and Baliphile, commissioned its creation while he was living in Bali during the 30s. The idea for the chorus was inspired by certain
trance dances in which a similar type of group male singing has an exor-
cistic role. Cak is still performed often, notably in the village of Bona, near
Gianyar, where it was first done. I Wayan Dibia, an important contemporary choreographer and author of a book on cak, took an interest in the
form during the early 1980s and devised several ingenious new versions of
it, one of which was designed to be enacted on Kuta beach at sunset. Tourists and villagers alike stared in fascination as the dancers, freed from the
confines of the normal performance arena, splashed through the water, the
cak rhythms blending seamlessly into the roar of the surf. Nowadays all
musicians know how "to cak" and sometimes integrate cak with gamelan
gong kebyar music, putting down their mallets for a passage and voicing
these rhythms instead.

Gamelan Miscellany

Our list of Balinese ensembles could easily be extended far beyond this
point, but a few additional lines will be made to suffice for the present.
There is *tektekan*, a form of baleganjur in which the cengceng are replaced

or augmented by bamboo sticks or wooden cowbells. Another "giant" gamelan of West Bali (cousin of the bamboo gamelan jegog) is the *kendang mabarung*, which features gargantuan drums carved in a single piece out of an entire tree trunk. The *gamelan batel*, a set of gender wayang instruments augmented with drums, cymbals and gongs, accompanies certain theatrical forms with stories drawn from the Ramayana epic. These include the *wayang wong* masked dance drama and some wayang kulit. *Cakepung*, a spontaneous and rowdy chorus in which voices imitate the different instruments of the gamelan, is popular in the northern and eastern parts of the island. One may encounter a *gong suling* ensemble, in which half a dozen or so suling of different sizes team up with gongs, cengceng and drums. And the *genggong*, a kind of jaw harp, performs in ensemble as accompaniment to a fairy-tale like dance about a frog-prince.

Balinese Vocal Genres

Unless accompanying a theatrical performance where actors speak and sing, most Balinese gamelan music is instrumental. But there is another world of musical activity closely connected to literature and scripture, where the teaching of morality, philosophy and music are intimately connected. This branch of Balinese music may find its audience in small and private gatherings, or in the inner spiritual world of a high priest in prayer, but is no less significant for not being intended to reach the general public.

The main function of singing in Bali—whether by a soloist or a chorus— is to give voice to classical poetic texts. Save for a few kinds of ancient ritual songs, poetry is written and preserved on lontar, leaves of the borassus palm (*borassus flabellifer*). Successive generations of Balinese scribes have continually recopied the works, introducing edits and changes commensurate with their historical or literary perspectives; few new poems in the classical forms are introduced today. The importance of vocal music lies as much with the literary meaning, linguistic conventions and performance context of the poems as it does with their melodic style and voice qualities of the singers. They are conceived of as literature to be "voiced," rather than as a separate aesthetic category of song, though musical detail receives more emphasis in some genres. In performance (a word perhaps only partially appropriate) the totality of features—language, content, timbre and intonation, and setting—are to be considered together.

Sloka are Sanskrit chants employed by *pedanda* (Brahman priests) during rituals and by puppeteers in the wayang kulit as invocations or to convene supernatural forces. A deep, chest-centered, guttural voice quality is used, intended to reverberate through and beyond the body. This is the only current usage of Sanskrit in Bali, and as such evokes the distant, quasi-mythological past of Hindu India. Sloka emphasize inherently charged syllables (such as *Ong* or *Aum*) that function as aural metaphors for cosmic unity. Rhythm is free, and melodies are syllabic, static and flat, constrained to at most three tones. Today few Balinese understand Sanskrit, but all can grasp that sloka are a channel linking the present to a sacred realm that transcends history, where mythic time converges with the supernatural forces sustaining the universe. Sloka was probably introduced to Bali during the first stages of Hindu influence, between the sixth and ninth centuries.

Kakawin are lengthy poems composed in Bali and Java beginning in the ninth century. They are written in the Old Javanese language *Kawi*, which is still widely known in Bali but rarely used or studied in Java. Kakawin poetic meters, based faithfully on Indian ones, are called *wirama* or known by the Javanese term *sekar ageng* (sekar here means meter; ageng is large or great). There are over 200 different types, each comprised of three or four line stanzas using a prescribed succession of long and short vowel sounds. There may be as many as 26 syllables in a line, and hundreds of stanzas in a complete text. Voice quality is commandingly deep and resonant.

Performance of kakawin is an intrinsically literary event, as they are usually vocalized in small gatherings of popular literary clubs called *sekaha pepaosan* (from *paos*, to read), where they are formally "performed," translated into vernacular Balinese, and interpreted for discussion. Kakawin literature, essentially extinct on Java, thrives in Bali through the *sekaha* pepaosan and represents an important link to the distant past for ordinary Balinese. Unlike the overtly philosophical and liturgical sloka, kakawin conjures up images of the deeds and beliefs of gods and ancestors, and thus has direct relevance for the teaching of morality in contemporary life.

Kidung, written in later forms of Javanese and Balinese, are indigenous Balinese narrative poems associated with the post-Majapahit era. Their subjects are the romances and battles of idealized, semi-fictional princely warriors such as the celebrated Panji. Kidung were composed in the palaces of the courts and in former times performed there by specialists in their interpretation; today there are still specialists and the music can be heard sung chorally by groups of worshippers at almost any type of Balinese ceremony.

Kidung poetic meters, called *sekar madya* (*madya* = medium), generally consist of pairs of double stanzas of unequal length. One characteristic type, Rara Kadiri, contains two stanzas of 80 syllables each, each ending with the vowel *a*, followed by two of 33 syllables, each ending with *i* (Wallis 1981:176). The vocal interpretation of kidung has historically been a confusing and difficult issue for both foreign and Balinese scholars. In general the poems are sung melismatically, proceeding slowly from syllable to syllable, with a much wider melodic range than kakawin. Kidung is of additional historical interest because at one time its performance was accompanied by the sacred *gamelan selunding*, gambang and luang, a connection that suggests a former integration of vocal and gamelan music on the island. As mentioned, this connection has been recently refortified by musician Wayan Sinti.

Geguritan is a poetic genre composed in Kawi or Balinese, with texts that are topical and far less connected to elite traditions than kidung. The meters used, called *pupuh* or *tembang*, are shorter and simpler than those of other poetry. Originating in Java, and known there as *tembang macapat* (or *sekar alit*), their presence on Bali predates that of kidung. They are very widespread, all the more so in the recent past because they are central to the performance of *arja* theater, a twentieth century form combining story, dance and singing. In arja, as in other Balinese theatrical genres, songs are associated with specific moods and character types. The actor-dancers must also be accomplished tembang singers.

Tembang meters are of many classifications, of which seven are in general use. Each has a fixed number of lines, syllables per line, and vowel ending for each line. Stanzaic forms have from 6–9 lines, and most lines have 8, 12 or 14 syllables. Singing style is throaty and highly ornamented with melisma, quick vibrato, and glissando. The *gamelan geguntangan*, used since the early 1900s to accompany arja performances, has drums, bamboo slit-gongs (*guntang*), and a suling as its only melodic instrument. Suling players are capable of nearly as much flexibility as the singers themselves and are expected to modify their playing to match singers' choice of intonations. These may vary from moment to moment due to improvisation or dramatic requirements. Among the most famous singers of pupuh are Ni Nyoman Canderi of Singapadu village and Cokorda Isteri Rai Partini of Peliatan. Singer Jero Suli of Kesiman village, beloved by audiences in the 1960s, was coaxed out of retirement in 1989 to record the well-known tembang Sinom Tamtam for track 11 of the book CD. Her voice exemplifies the tense timbre, fluid rhythm and highly ornamented melody that define the style.

In the past thirty years there has been renewed interest in the singing of poetry. Most villages now have special groups for the study and performance of kakawin and kidung at ceremonies, and children are especially encouraged to join. There are even competitions to choose the groups with the best technique and deportment. In addition, composers have recently created gamelan forms (*gegitaan* and *sandya gita*) that integrate the singing of texts into new instrumental compositions. Many such pieces are arranged for soloists and chorus with gamelan gong kebyar, and included in the annual Festival Gong competitions.

There is plentiful vocal music that does not fit any of the categories just described, including children's songs and song-games (see Chapter Seven) and songs used to accompany exorcist trance ceremonies and dances (*gending sanghyang*). The latter, heard mostly in northeastern Bali Aga villages where such ceremonies likely originated, appear to be among the oldest types of music—of any kind—on the island.

Gamelan gender wayang batel at a temple ceremony in Mas village.

Music in
Balinese Society

Just east of Rendang, a village in Karangasem district on the way to Besakih temple, there is a southward turnoff that leads onto a gravelly, unpaved
road. The terrain is fairly flat but it rains almost every day in this part of
Bali, and after a downpour the mud makes everything slippery. The three or
four kilometer ride down the path to the village of Segah is treacherous on
such days, and the village, once reached, does not extend any overt greet-
ings to visitors. Tin roofs, scraggly dogs, a soccer field, and a few idlers
chatting over coffee at a roadside stand all seem insignificant below the
breathtaking vista of Mount Agung, which towers imposingly to the north.

   At the south end of the village, under an open pavilion with a thatched
roof and cement floor, a *gamelan* is rehearsing. The instrument cases, never
having been carved for lack of funds and painted in swaths of brilliant red
and green, have been fairly well devoured by termites, although the bronze
keys and gongs sound good. The musicians, 30 of them or so, are dressed
in T-shirts and woven sarongs. They are hemmed in on all sides by gawkers
who crowd in so close that the players around the edges can barely move
their mallets. Even though the musicians and the spectators work in the
same ricefields together, those that belong to the gamelan group acquire
a special aura when they make music that makes them worthy of their co-
villagers prolonged stares of fascination and appreciation.

In the middle sits Windha, a composer teaching the group a new piece that they have requested from him. It is now 4 p.m. and he has been working with them without a break since 11 in the morning, going bit by bit through the music, starting at the beginning and adding more as the players can absorb it. He is patient and exacting but the music is full of complex melodies, *kotekan* and drumming. The piece is beautiful and intricately patterned in a way that sets the ordinariness of the villagers learning it in sharp and surprising relief. The musicians, down to the last player, are in a state of rapt concentration, and even though Windha does not assert himself very aggressively there is order, cooperation and discipline at the rehearsal. Nevertheless, some passages just prove to be too hard. The spell breaks when the *reyong* players make a noticeable mistake, and chaos ensues. Some continue playing heedlessly, others wipe their brows in resignation and then launch into an entirely different part of the piece, still more yell at each other in a crossfire of criticisms and exasperated complaints. Windha sits quietly in the center and gives a time-out sign.

"*Ning no ning nong, ni nong ni no ning no ning,*" he sings, "Keep the tempo steady on the reyong!"

The reyong players try it again and again, failing utterly. All eyes are upon them. At first they are embarrassed and simper, but soon they collapse in each other's arms, laughing hysterically at themselves. They have everyone's sympathy now, so the tension abates.

"What's my part in the intro to the *gangsa kotekan*?" one of the *jegogan* players interjects. Windha demonstrates on the instrument closest to him. The jegogan players copy him, and soon the *gangsa* section enters with the kotekan. The reyong, meantime, is still intent on perfecting the passage they were working on, and the drummers have begun to argue over the details of one of their rhythms. The din quickly becomes unbearable.

"Quiet", says Windha in an unusually forceful tone, "Let's take it again from the beginning."

Balinese Musical Organizations

The atmosphere at the rehearsal in Segah typifies that of rehearsals that take place all the time in any of the thousands of Balinese villages with active gamelan. By dint of concentrated effort, Balinese musicians learn an art of technical rigor and esthetic power, aid in fulfilling the ritual needs of a community totally dependent on the proper placation of its deities, and play a vital role in civic life. Almost never do they earn any substantial income from music. Being a musician is primarily a voluntary public activity, centered around a communal space: the *balai banjar*, or community meeting hall. Here is where the instruments are kept, where the group meets and rehearses, and in many instances, where it performs too. People gather at the balai banjar to play gamelan for the pleasure of working hard together with their co-villagers to make something artistically satisfying and then enjoying the pride and sense of accomplishment of having done so. Making music without the challenges and rewards of group effort would be considered a pointless and unfulfilling chore to a Balinese.

The gamelan organization is only one of a roster of formally established groups, or *sekaha* (pronounced s'-kha), that operate out of each *banjar*. Some are a part of every banjar's organization and mandate the participation of at least one person from many of the households in the community, such as the rice harvesting sekaha. Some are voluntary but have equally practical goals, such as bicycle repair or computer technicians' sekaha. Others vary from village to village and are often so whimsical in purpose that one wonders why there is a need for any kind of formal structure or charter such as the banjar demands, like the kite flying sekaha. Why, one might ask, can't the people who like to fly kites just get together if the wind is blowing? It's just not right, and not nearly as enjoyable, answer the Balinese, unless there's a sekaha. The matrix of sekaha stipulates each individual's role in the life of the banjar and shapes the varied personalities in the community into a single, complex, functioning whole.

Whether or not the nature of Balinese music developed from these social circumstances or the circumstances were influenced by the music is moot. In any case they are ideally suited for one another. The close coordination between the gamelan's melodic parts and the interlocking of the kotekan demand a close interaction between the players during rehearsal that is analogous to the larger structure of the society. The music requires a collective memory and a group instinct that is a natural outgrowth of the musicians' proximity to each other in daily life. *Gotong royong*, the practice of mutual help, comes first, and good music follows naturally.

Belonging to the *gamelan sekaha* is a coveted privilege. As many as 75 people may take part, although only half of those can be accommodated as players at any one time. Others are understudies, administrators, instrument maintainers, treasurers, and costume designers. When wealthy business-men in Banjar Kalah, at the south end of Peliatan village, contributed a gamelan to the banjar organization in March 1989, over 80 people signed up to join the sekaha immediately. Rehearsals had to be planned in shifts for a while so that everyone got a chance to play. A natural filtering-out process ensued in which those with greater enthusiasm and talent sought out per-manent places in the ensemble; others dropped out or found other ways to be part of the sekaha. Before a premiere performance was even envisioned, a group of teenage boys threw themselves into the week-long production of an elaborate stage backdrop for the instruments. Give a new gamelan to a banjar, and watch the community come glowingly to life.

Teachers and the Learning Process
When a banjar acquires a gamelan it does two things right away: set up the administrative apparatus to support a sekaha, and search for an auspicious day on the Balinese calendar to have the gamelan blessed and activities inaugurated. Once this is taken care of, a teacher must be procured, for the group cannot proceed without one. If there is no one knowledgeable within the banjar, arrangements are made for an outsider to be brought in.

If the teacher is a performing member of the group, he sits himself be-hind the lead drum at rehearsals. If not, he takes a place in the center that is visible to all. To start he approaches one of the gangsa in the front row and plays through a section of the piece to be taught, gesturing the gongs and *kempli* into motion at the right times. Before he has even played a few notes, the group begins to imitate him—blindly and cacophonously at first, but after a while the sound comes into focus. The musicians learn both by listening to what he plays and, just as importantly, by watching the direc-tion his mallet takes across the keys. They memorize the music as a group, instinctively reacting to and correcting each other. After some time, the teacher moves over to the reyong and drums and demonstrates their parts. As the music cycles around, the core melody instruments can usually derive their own parts from what the gangsa play. If individual players are having trouble they are given special attention, or simply allowed to falter on the assumption that, in time, the music will 'enter them'.

A brand new group needs time to master the technique of damping the

The teacher demonstrates the melodies and patterns to be learned on the instrument closest to him.

keys. To this end, a simple piece like a gilak ostinato may be played over and over again for days or weeks until the sound is clear and articulate. An established group, experienced in learning together, may bite off a substantial chunk of music at a sitting, spending most of the rehearsal time working out details of dynamics, tempo and angsel. Before long they can play even the most demanding music with verve and conviction.

It is impossible to imagine gamelan players reading from a musical score or parts the way Western musicians do, even though it is quite possible to write the music down. Reading music is a process of translating symbols into sounds; Balinese musicians bypass this stage entirely and learn music by transforming a received musical gesture directly into the physical act of playing. Correspondingly, in most gamelan music the variety of different kinds of musical patterns, while infinite, is somewhat more limited than it would be in a tradition where music is normally notated and composers are free to invent things that need not be memorized. Although each gamelan piece is unique, the instruments each have their roles, melodies have recognizable forms, and there are only so many different styles of kotekan. This partially explains how Balinese musicians can ingest such great amounts of music. On the other hand, there is no explanation for the breadth of some

players' memories. Many can access any of hundreds of tunes and their accompanying parts, some of which they may not have recalled for years, in a
brief instant. Yet what has just been said applies equally to older traditional
repertoires and to much recent music, which may use nontraditional musical
patterning so complex and transforming as to seem to defy memorization.

Traditionally, a new gamelan's first task has been to learn the repertoire
of *lelamhatan* needed for temple ceremonies, for a sekaha's central purpose
is to fulfill ritual needs. Simultaneously they learn the music needed to accompany the *topeng* (masked dance) play as this also has religious associations. Then it is up to the group to decide which, if any, kinds of secular
music appeal to them, taking into account the types of performances that
are likely to generate some income for the sekaha treasury. Gamelan without such ambitious plans will learn enough repertoire to be able to provide
unremunerated entertainment within their own village when it is called for.
In South Bali, however, many sekaha assemble *tari lepas* performances in
the hope of procuring a regular, paying engagement playing for tourists. In
outlying areas it can be profitable to hook up with a company of actors and
singers to perform various kinds of theatrical shows *(drama gong*, topeng,
arja and *prembon* are among the genres), given with full musical accompaniment, that Balinese audiences flock to see. When a sekaha does earn
money, only a very insignificant percentage, if any, goes into the players'
pockets. Most goes into the treasury. The members earn their sustenance
from other jobs, complementing it with the recognition and satisfaction that
comes from being part of a gamelan group.

The economy of being a Balinese gamelan teacher has modern and traditional aspects. As conservatory teachers or when training musicians in
official capacities—such as for government-sponsored festivals, music
teachers are salaried. But in the village and banjar system they are rarely
paid in cash; at that level Balinese find it awkward or inappropriate to attempt to fix a monetary value for the transmission of musical knowledge.
The process of payment is instead more complex and involves establishing
a relationship that cannot be neatly terminated once the teacher completes
his professional obligations to the group. For years to come the group members will shower special favors on him, bringing food to his home before
a feast or providing a team of carpenters and free labor if part of his home
needs renovation. Many teachers will beam with pride in explaining that

they have never once been so crass as to ask for any kind of payment, and then go on to describe all the various kinds of compensation that have been voluntarily given by students in expression of their gratitude and respect.

Children and Music

Children in Bali begin their musical education at an early age. Since gamelan instruments are kept in the balai banjar, they are accessible not just to the members of the sekaha, but to the community at large. When rehearsals take place they are open to all, and children are encouraged to attend. Those who have a parent playing in the group can often be seen sitting on their fathers' laps watching and listening intently. Others crowd around the edge of the rehearsal space. After rehearsal and during the mornings, kids return to bang out their own improvisational approximations of what they have heard. No parent ever directs their child to study music or to take lessons, and there are no scales to practice or exercises to master. It is not necessary to purchase an instrument for home study or to make any kind of investment. Children who evince a serious interest simply progress on their own from crude mimicking to careful imitation to the thorough absorption of the actual repertoire, all of which is solidly reinforced by constant exposure to the adult group's music making.

In addition to nurturing physical dexterity and sensitive musicianship, as a large group activity gamelan is also an ideal laboratory for developing discipline, cooperation and other social skills that will go a long way towards helping young Balinese grow into productive members of their society. As an educational environment there is little that could surpass it. When young Balinese learn music, they also come into contact with dance, theater, puppetry, mythology and literature, experiencing through direct participation the matrix of artistic activities that their traditional life cultivates. Even at the youngest of ages they are made aware of the great importance attached to music. From birth onward babies are fêted with a series of prescribed religious ceremonies that utilize gamelan, and soon thereafter they become aware of the continuous presence of gamelan at ceremonies of all kinds, both within the temples and without. When they are old enough to want to try the instruments out for themselves, there is no discouragement, intimidation, or inference that making music is an activity reserved for a privileged few. There are only the instruments, other similarly inclined

Children begin their musical education in informal imitation of their elders.

playmates, and the beginnings of the life-long practice of the music itself.

Music is often a family affair. Some families have artistic blood going back for generations and even venerate their inherited talent with a *balai taksu*, a special shrine for *taksu* (performance charisma) in their temple. Children in these homes are flooded with musical stimuli from birth and are often expert drummers or *gender* players from an early age. The sense of dedication is terrific: Wayan Suweca of Denpasar talks of having taken his drum to bed with him every night during his childhood, waking up each morning to begin the day by practicing before a mirror to refine posture and facial expression. Now he, along with three brothers and sisters, are among the best known musicians in Bali.

In the 1930s, Colin McPhee presented a *gamelan angklung* to the children in the village of Sayan. He wrote about their rapid evolution from being a bunch of ordinary children to being in demand as a serious organization of skilled musicians in *A Club of Small Men* and *Children and Music in Bali*. Today organized children's sekaha are commonplace. It is uncanny to witness the earnestness and precision with which such groups, made up of children ages 7-17, play the same difficult pieces that their elders play. Some young musicians are barely able to get their hands around both ends of a drum before they can perform with an assurance that belies their age.

Very young Balinese have their own musical domain in the *dolanan*, or children's songs and song-games, of which there are hundreds. Some of these are found Bali-wide; others are known only in certain villages or regions. There are nonsense songs, clapping games, lullabies, and melodies with movements or activities tied to them. As is true nearly everywhere, internet, television and radio are having their deleterious effect on the popularity of these songs, but they are still an important pastime and a good way of learning social and musical skills for Bali's children.

Late Twentieth Century Developments

There is evidence that in the 19th century Bali concubines played music in royal palaces. But for most of the 20th century the only place for women in Balinese musical life was either as a singer—in the temple or as a character actress in a dramatic performance—or as a performer in the informal *oncang-oncangan*, a kind of music made from the interlocking sounds of bamboo poles striking the ground during rice husking. Women's roles in traditional artistic life were generally restricted to dancing, weaving and the making of offerings. Men monopolized the plastic arts of painting and carving, shared the dance stage with women, and played gamelan.

In the 1970s things began to change. In 1979 the first women puppeteers performed, and at around the same time a few female music majors enrolled at the conservatory. Two of these, Ketut Suryatini and Desak Made Laksmi, joined the faculty after they graduated. In the early 1980s the first all-female *gong kebyar sekaha* were founded and later included, along with men's gamelan, into the yearly Festival Gong gamelan competitions. In keeping with the regulations of the festival, every year a different group from each of Bali's eight districts must enter, so that by now several dozen women's gamelan have been formed. Some disband soon after the competitions, having no ambitions beyond the goal of competing. Others, such as one in Peliatan village, grew into mature organizations that maintain a regular performance schedule.

The experience of playing gamelan is as new for the women doing it as it is for the people who come to see it. Some explain the changes as a consequence of foreign influence, as Balinese have come in contact with international gamelan students of both sexes, and asked themselves "why not?"

Thus far there have only been short-lived mixed-gender groups, but as the notion of women musicians becomes more familiar, some may emerge. These sorts of changes take root slowly. The women's groups are of secular origin and few have penetrated the surface of the Balinese social structure. If they do, girls will receive the same encouragement to play music in the banjar that boys do, and women's musicianship will be cultivated in a vital way, incorporated into the communal and religious life of the village.

Gamelan festival competitions, an important forum for women musicians, have long been a fixture in Balinese musical life. The first ones were held every few years during the 30s and 40s; since the late 1970s they have been taking place every May and June without fail. In March or early April, the eight regional governments each select one women's and one men's group from their district as representatives. Teams of locally-based coaches and teachers are sent to the chosen villages regularly to help with the rehearsals, which commence upon a group's selection and continue daily for two months. Competition guidelines clearly delineate what must be prepared: typically (although it changes somewhat from year to year) one lelambatan, one *kreasi baru* instrumental piece, two classical dances, one new choreography, and one choral piece with full gamelan accompaniment. Then in late May, a committee of experts is sent by the government arts council to see a full rehearsal and give suggestions and comments.

During the first two weeks of June the competition is held. The atmosphere at these events is much more reminiscent of a sporting event than a concert. Outside the performance area vendors set up all manner of wares from coffee and cakes to toys from Hong Kong. The crowd overflows from the auditorium, usually a roofed pavilion with no walls, and spills out into the streets and up palm trees and walls. The audiences are thoroughly responsive to everything taking place in the music or dance, reacting instantaneously with approving cheers at a particularly well-executed passage, or jeering with abandon at the slightest mistake. (At one such concert in Amlapura in 1977, a missed jegogan tone brought 3,000 people to their feet in a spontaneous chorus of boos.) Through the hubbub, the jury members calmly make notes on their little pads, voting on 1st and 2nd place winners once they have seen all of the performances. Fierce regional pride is invoked, and audience accusations of juror bias and favoritism of some regions over others are common. The political dimensions get intense as local governments come under pressure to offer more financial and material support to their representative groups.

The yearly Festival Gong and Bali Arts Festival, the constant stream of musical performances emanating from the conservatories, and the ever-increasing number of village sekaha with regular work performing for tourists, have created a broader range of contexts for gamelan in secular life than has heretofore been known in Bali. This has often had the effect of strengthening the sacred ties which are the root of the tradition, simply because there are more sekaha available and eager to play their part in rituals.

At the same time, many young Balinese, bombarded by a hail of outside influences resulting from Indonesia's increasing international presence, the influx of tourists, foreign goods and Western culture, and of course the digital world, are perhaps less aware than ever of the history and diversity of their own music. As one journalist wrote in the Bali Post, "Ask a young teenager in Denpasar the meaning of the terms *semar pegulingan, gong gdé* or *gambuh* and they will shrug their shoulders in ignorance." Whether or not that is an exaggeration, it is certainly indicative of the struggle that a dynamic and changing society like Bali's must undergo in order to maintain its identity.

CHAPTER EIGHT

Three Generations
of Balinese Musicians

In Bali few individual musicians emerge as stars in their own right. The interlocking, cooperative levels of Balinese society and their reflection in the making of music work to discourage this. On the whole it is the *sekaha* that achieve recognition, especially those that have noteworthy accomplishments to their credit, have attained a markedly high level of musicianship, or are the preservers of an unusual style or form. However Balinese society is also strongly marked by hierarchy and prestige, and increasingly, players of extraordinary ability and personality do gain fame as teachers and disseminators. Bali is small enough to ensure that their numbers are comparatively few and their milieus interconnected. The tone of Balinese musical life is set by this community, whose members circulate among the village groups of the island directing, coaching and lending their expertise whenever their skills are requested. The efforts and aspirations of these artists make them the role models that younger Balinese musicians look up to. Their work steers a course for the development and regeneration of the tradition.

The three musicians profiled in the following pages were chosen with difficulty since so many of their gifted colleagues had to be excluded. As a trio they represent a cross-section of the musical community in terms of age, experience and outlook. All exerted strong influence on Balinese music in the late 20th century by being affiliated with an important village group or institution. The first one, I Wayan Tembres, represents the increasingly rare breed of unschooled and thoroughly traditional musicians that made their lives in music as teachers and performers in village groups. Now quite old, the profile below depicts him during the peak years of his musical life in the 1960s–90s, but his comments are as meaningful now as they were during that time. The second, I Madé Bandem, is an influential academic with an international reputation who has had an extraordinary career; his thoughts reflect decades of dwelling in the corridors of cultural influence and power. Last, I Dewa Ketut Alit, a performer and composer now in his thirties, explains his perspective on musical values, creativity, and the challenges confronting the culture of *gamelan* now. Profile of a fourth musician, I Wayan Suweca, comes at the close of Chapter Ten.

I Wayan Tembres

As one of the senior statesmen of Balinese gamelan, Wayan Tembres personified the village teacher. Carrying on the time-honored practice of offering his skills to villages desirous of forming or improving a sekaha, Tembres, during the past fifty years, established a broad network of disciples and colleagues throughout the island. Cheerfully contradicting the archetype of the venerable and inscrutable guru, Tembres is beloved for his playful, witty, and humble demeanor, and the burning musical energy he so effortlessly shared. Even as an *empu* (revered older artist) he always exuded the spirit of a man half his age.

Tembres is from Blangsinga, about 1 kilometer south of Blahbatuh village. With its heritage of courtly arts, this culturally vibrant region provided a fertile environment for his training. Like most aspiring musicians in Bali, Tembres hardly ever had one-to-one study with elder musicians. Rather he learned by tagging along with his father Pareg, a *rebab* and *suling* player at the court (right up until his death in 1991 at over 90 years of age, he made hand-carved suling daily), and by absorbing and imitating the music he heard all around him.

Best known as a drummer with an incisive attack and unwavering rhythm, his presence at the helm of a gamelan inspired calm and assurance in his fellow musicians and brought out verve and intensity in dancers. His small, strong hand cut through musical time like a knife on the drum skins, and his

I Wayan Tembres

unmistakable drumming groove was instantly recognizable and never suc-
cesfully imitated. Tembres' most famous students are the sekaha from Pindha
village (see page 90) on the road south of Blangsinga. During the '60s, he
steered them towards their participation and near-triumph in the 1969 Festival Gong. The event was one of the climactic points of his career:

"I was scheduled to play drum for Pindha against the Geladag group at
an amphitheater in Bangli. That day I had been taken to Denpasar by mo-
torbike to arrange my official papers for a gamelan tour to Teheran that I
was departing with the next week. On the way back to Bangli we had an
accident. I passed out and came to disoriented and bloody. Nevertheless I
insisted on getting to the performance area so I could formally request per-
mission not to play. But when I got there the group wouldn't hear of it; they
were scared to go on without me. I was covered with bandages but I had
to acquiesce. It was my condition that caused me to miss some key *angsel*
that night, and the audience practically rioted on account of my mistakes.
The whole situation was out of control, but I kept playing. The jury had to
give us second place but I got plenty of recognition for my endurance and
dedication.

"The Pindha group has been very strong and its reputation is secure. I
could be critical and even show some anger when I worked with them because they already have the skills they need and should not shirk from ap-
plying those skills. They are disciplined and absolutely uniform and that is
the key to playing well. But I believe that in teaching beginners one must
cajole, joke, and above all be patient. Once they know the music, then you
can proceed in earnest. That's where the real work begins.

"Music entails being sensitive to signals from musicians, dancers, and especially from the audience. The drummer can use his craft to enliven any
performance at which the audience shows signs of boredom. If the dancer is
acting forlorn, cue a few surprise angsel! If the musicians' concentration wa-
vers, pull up the tempo a bit. That snaps them back to attention every time.

"I taught myself to play the *kendang* by listening to other players and fig-
uring out what they did as best I could. But finally I had to create my own
style. The village atmosphere is good for that kind of learning. Students
who now do well at KOKAR and ISI should remember that they could
never have made it there without the kind of training they got at home.

"Some things are more difficult for musicians now than they used to be, and some are better. When I was young school and outside pressures were not present to keep my friends and me from playing music all day every day. Now, obviously, it's harder for young people to find that much time for gamelan, unless they enter a conservatory. But the ones that are serious play very well. Music is just as well-performed today as it ever was.

"I have never asked for money as a teacher. It's not right to do so. The rewards come to you anyhow, in other ways. We get a token fee for performing in the hotels now that we never used to get, but it's not enough for anyone to consider that a reason for doing those performances. We do them for the activity and the challenge, and for the strength of the sekaha organization. In the temples, of course, it's our duty to play for free and it always will be. No one fails to meet those obligations, and that's why our tradition is so strong."

Dr. Madé Bandem

Foremost among Bali's cultural disseminators is Dr. Madé Bandem, long-time head of the ISI academy in Denpasar. Bandem's guidance was essential to the development of the school ever since its founding in the 1960s. After leaving that post in 1997 he took up a deanship at Gajah Madah University in Java, and subsequently taught in the USA. Trained primarily as a dancer, but also skilled as a musician and very active as a scholar, Bandem's influence is strongly felt not only within the school but throughout the island and amongst ethnomusicologists worldwide.

Bandem was born in 1945. His father, the late I Madé Keredek, was a renowned dancer and literary scholar from Singapadu village. During the first half of the 20th century Keredek was instrumental in the development of several important theatrical forms, supporting his creativity with a pronounced intellectual energy that his son thoroughly absorbed. As a member of one of the conservatories' first graduating classes, Bandem was involved in the inception of the *sendratari* music/dance/drama form, a performance genre that has since demonstrated a staying power and ability to absorb influences of other styles akin to *kebyar* in its vitality. He performed widely during his youth as a dancer and was a member of several cultural missions abroad, including one to Beijing in 1963. He spent much of the late 60s and 70s as a student in the United States, ultimately obtaining a Ph.D. in ethnomusicology from Wesleyan University.

Dr. Madé Bandem

The rapid ascendance of ISI as a center for Balinese music and dance and the larger questions that arise when the school's pivotal role in the overall cultural scene are examined form the core of Bandem's commentary on his work and aspirations:

"The Balinese are a very tolerant and creative people. What this in effect means for our performing arts is that absorption of outside influences and internal growth move at a rate much too quick for us to document and codify completely. Each generation of musicians in our society will have a markedly different history from its predecessors and successors. We are very fast to learn but never satisfied to simply receive knowledge as presented; we feel compelled to interpret and modify it. At ISI and elsewhere we record, videotape and write about changes in our music with diligence and thoroughness, but none of these activities have the same intrinsic value as the kind of living documentation—namely, the very process of learning, creating and performing our music—that needs to be emphasized most.

"I am aware of how distinct our creative process is from that of the West, and I like these differences very much. In the West there is a focus on the individual and the potential for unique and original artistry. In Bali what we have is a shared pool of cultural resources that all of our artists tap into and take from instinctively. We don't really have breaks with the past or drastic changes, instead we have transformation, ornamentation, development. Almost all of our new music is based on classical models. This is an important concept.

"For the greater part of our recorded history we have been isolated in Bali. For almost 500 years no one disturbed us. Our kings and our gods were unquestioned sources of authority and wisdom and the benevolent presiders over the growth of our arts. Hindu culture was preserved and confined in Bali and to this day the Balinese do not want to change this any more than is necessary. They have been peaceful and feel no need to revolutionize or sever ties.

"Kebyar is still developing and will probably not decline in popularity for some time to come because of its musical flexibility and the freedom with which it can be used. Seven-tone and other older gamelan may revive but all of these have specific ritual connotations whereas kebyar from the very first was intended exclusively for artistic presentation. There were over 1500 active kebyar groups in Bali the last time the Ministry of Culture took a census, and there are probably more that are dormant. The profusion is delightful.

"We have a responsibility at ISI to be involved in the upholding of artistic standards, particularly where tourist performances are concerned. Many groups are overworked—some perform nightly—and are not always able to do their best. We initiated a program to have our students and graduates help to organize the village groups and negotiate on their behalf with hotel managers for reasonable performance schedules. We also like to see some graduates employed as artistic directors at the hotels themselves, where they organize the music and dance programs and work to educate visitors about what is presented.

"There are more musicians in Bali now that think of themselves as professionals in a way that was not so in the past. These artists are well positioned to play a major role in our international relations. More and more are able to earn their livelihood from music. We have more cultural missions and teachers going abroad, study programs for foreign students, gamelan shipped overseas—all of which makes our musicians proud and gives them work too! Cultural exchange raises the musicians' quality of life and by example provides motivation for younger generations.

"There is nothing that Bali is more proud of than her arts, and music and dance are the most expressive of these. Through them, Westerners will know the Balinese mind, soul and personality. They will be our connection to the rest of the world. And since music has universal meanings as well as culturally specific ones, no one will deny us our pride. Rather, they will seek to understand us better."

I Dewa Ketut Alit

Dewa Ketut Alit is a distinguished contemporary composer, born into a family of musicians and visual artists in Pengosekan village in 1973. Intensely serious and graced with a unique musical intelligence, Alit is a dynamic conversationalist willing to go the distance to pursue ideas, musical or otherwise. He has taught extensively around the world (the U.S., Canada, Australia, Japan), produced fusion compositions with musicians abroad, and heard his work presented in prestigious concert halls in each place. To be sure, in Bali Alit is celebrated for his innovations within traditional gamelan. The gorgeous Geregel (2000) and the rhythmically labyrinthine Caru Wara (2005) are good examples. But as of 2010 he was moving far beyond this in works like Salju (Snow) and Es (Ice), which, as their titles suggest, are so otherworldly and abstracted from conventional gamelan sound as to be barely recognizable as such. Still, they are profoundly musical.

Musicians in Alit's generation were in their impressionable twenties in 1998, when Indonesia started moving towards fuller democracy and accountability in government. What did such momentous changes at the top mean for musicians "on the street"? In Alit's case, it prompted him to give strong voice to criticisms and dissatisfactions that his elders would have kept closer to the chest. He almost surely could have had a safer career as a conservatory teacher, but decisively elected not to so he could pursue life as an independent artist and remain, true to his forebears, an activist for arts in his village. Though his thinking and his music evince a canny global awareness, he is grateful to tradition and knows full well that he stands on its shoulders.

"As a kid I simply loved gamelan and was intensely motivated to be the best musician I possibly could. All three of my brothers felt the same, and we had our father as a model. In Pengosekan at that time music was so

I Dewa Ketut Alit

alive. My dad's *arja* group—arja was his specialty—practiced almost every day. His drumming partner for that was Madé Lebah, such an eminent, graceful and beautiful player, and so legendary. We called him *kak* (grandfather). Just across the road at the *banjar*, my dad was lead drummer for Tunas Mekar, the *gong kebyar* group.[1] There were always performances going on, including many for tourists. When I was about 10, going into grade 4, my older brother Dewa Putu organized a new Tunas Mekar for the younger generation. We got chosen to play in the Festival Gong in 1987 and that eventually inspired my brothers and me to found Sanggar Çudamani [see Chapter Ten] which brought musical life in Pengosekan to a whole new level.

"I've seen a lot of musical change as an adult, and I've composed a lot of new music, some of it, I admit, pretty unusual. I always think about the rela-

---

1 Alit's father Dewa Nyoman Sura is the drummer on the right in the photo of Tunas Mekar on pages ii–iii (color inserts). Aside from being renowned as a performer and teacher, Madé Lebah (~1912–1996), from neighboring Peliatan, was Colin McPhee's guide and chauffeur in the 1930s.

tionship between the tradition that shaped me and the modern artistic free-
doms I have. We are so free with our music today, but the tradition created
us and we always have to remember that in the end it is wiser than we are.
I've taught gamelan all over the world. From this I have come to know my
own music outside of the traditional context that built me up—ironically, to
the point where I can sometimes leave it and get to see it from the outside.
I've begun to see how there might be a new, broader conception of what
gamelan is, one based on its relationship to other cultures.

"After composing so much in Bali, and after listening to all kinds of music
all over the world—in Japan, Canada, the U.S.A.—my musical imagination
has taken me places I never dreamed I would go. I hear all kinds of things in
my mind—changing waves of patterns, multiple melodies running at different speeds and always changing their relationship to one another. The music
is in me but I am still straining to bring it out. I feel that my music is an
extension of the tradition but not everyone can hear it this way. Sometimes
I can't even really explain what I want to the musicians who come to play
with me. But it is coming, slowly.

"I am aware that my musical values are always changing, and that they
are changing me. Still, there are some underlying ones that do not change.
One is that there has to be artistic discipline, which I see as the need for the
musician to find the sole right path that will lead him to the musical goal or
object sought. And there must be a human awareness: humility before other
musicians and our art, mutual love and respect.

"There are good and difficult aspects to being a Balinese musician today,
and to the condition of Balinese music generally. We do care for our music
and its roots in religion. Gamelan is acknowledged as an important part of
the Balinese character; that is, people understand that to play when young
is enriching and part of growing up to be a responsible adult. These ideas
command respect everywhere. And I am happy to be able to say that after
a period when formal education and the culture of ISI seemed to be a little
too dominant in musical life, we're now seeing a lot more artistic autonomy
and empowerment in the villages.

"The problems trouble me. People don't realize how much the government bureaucracy and business manipulate us, without our individual interests at heart, and rarely with the needs and concerns of village traditions in
mind. Politicking and extraneous needs sometimes determine which groups

get selected for this or that festival, tour or event. In a way this is our own fault too. There's a certain lack of thoughtfulness when it comes to purely artistic things. Some young musicians are trapped in "tourist performance syndrome". Leaving aside the question of the quality of these performances, this has a tendency to foster some cynicism about one's own culture: that it's for sale, that performing is no big deal or just a "gig", and so on. Musicians need to be aware—they can't just be passive recipients of music any more, but need to take hold of the issues confronting us, get into some serious dialogue about where we are going. We haven't yet had a serious music critic in Bali. We need some, and we need everyone to think, to help raise consciousness of what we are and where we are headed."

CHAPTER NINE

Getting Involved

Balinese music is a tradition of extraordinary vitality and a source of pride for the Balinese. The centuries of cultural isolation that Bali experienced prior to the 20th century served to fortify the social and religious roles of *gamelan* music to such an extent that the rapid influx of foreign ideas that besiege Bali today are perceived mostly as a stimulus to musical development rather than a threat. In no way can it be said that the tradition is ossified; in fact, as we have seen, there is more music and musical creativity in Bali today than ever before.

Today, all over the world people's musical tastes and listening habits are infinitely broader than they were. But as recently as a few decades ago only the most progressive or adventurous of musicians sought direct interaction with other musical cultures. With the exception of a handful of ethnographers, most outsiders exposed to gamelan music in the past experienced it as an exotic phenomenon and did not pursue it beyond that. Of course, the music was not nearly as accessible then as it is today. And now hundreds of thousands of visitors come to Bali yearly and hear gamelan music as a matter of course during their stay. Among them are many foreign students who come with the express purpose of learning to play gamelan instruments either in the villages from local teachers or, more formally, at the conservatory. Gamelan from Bali perform abroad regularly and many sets of instruments have found their way to other countries, where interested people study the music either from experienced non-Balinese or directly from native teachers. Balinese musicians teaching abroad may be part of the Indonesian diplomatic service or they may, as is sometimes the case with conservatory faculty, be pursuing advanced degrees in ethnomusicology or a related subject at foreign universities.

For Balinese musicians involved in such developments, these are encouraging processes that merit full support. As Dr. Bandem noted in the previous chapter, the arts are the primary medium through which the Balinese can establish a meaningful connection with the world at large. Foreigners who evince an interest in gamelan music are therefore met with respect and appreciation by musicians on the island. Such interactions are tangible proof of the esteem in which gamelan music is held internationally, which in turn further reinforces the importance of cultivating the music for the Balinese themselves.

Musical Performances

Most foreigners who arrive in Bali for a brief stay encounter gamelan in performance at hotels. There are many *sekaha* whose home villages are situated in reasonable proximity to tourist-concentrated areas that have regular contractual engagements to offer a selection of music and dance pieces on stages set up at the hotels themselves; others perform daily or weekly in their villages at *balai banjar* outfitted with chairs and lighting for a bussed-in audience. All of these performances are regulated by the government arts council LISTIBIYA, which auditions and certifies the groups for quality and authenticity.

Many programs of this type offer an opening instrumental composition followed by a welcoming dance, derived from a sacred temple dance, in which pairs of female dancers make offerings and strew the audience with flower petals as a gesture of greeting. Thereupon follows a mixed selection of *tari lepas kebyar*-style dances, some classical masked dances or a Baris, and perhaps even a Legong. Some groups, notably the ones that perform in Batubulan village, present more elaborate theatrical pieces that involve the protector-dragon Barong and its nemesis, the witch Rangda. This last, which is extremely sacred in origin and fraught with dangerous magical connotations in its original temple setting, has been altered and condensed

Offerings are made before every performance.

so as to render it appropriate for recreational presentation. Nevertheless, before these and all gamelan performances, a priest is summoned to bless the performance area, musicians, dancers and instruments, and to propitiate any malevolent forces that might conspire to disrupt or otherwise adversely affect the presentation.

Groups engaged to perform in hotels are usually hired for a set fee, out of which musicians' and dancers' honorariums and other expenses including costumes, maintenance and transportation must be paid. The performers end up with very little in their pockets—normally less than a few dollars per performance—but the steadiness of the work does provide a supplement to whatever other sources of income they have. On performance days a truck is hired and at about 6 p.m. the sekaha members appear on the roadside in their village waiting to be picked up. They load the heavy gamelan instruments into the bed of the truck, pile in with it and head towards the hotel, their multi-colored musician's uniforms drawing stares and cheers from bystanders along the road.

Other Venues for Hearing Music
While hotel performances are mostly of high quality, they can only give an inkling of the experience that Balinese music offers in its natural envi-

ronment at temples in villages around the island. Temple anniversary ceremonies, known as *odalan*, are almost always underway somewhere. Visitors are welcome and encouraged to attend these events, with the essential stipulations that full Balinese temple dress be worn and that the progress of the ceremony not be disturbed. (Most Balinese contact, guide or hotel employee can provide information on where odalan are taking place at any given time and give instruction on matters of clothing and etiquette.) The best time to hear music at a temple ceremony is in the late afternoon and early evening, when offerings are brought in to the accompaniment of *lelambatan*, *gamelan angklung*, or other gamelan that a village may maintain. After hours there is often a complete dance or theatrical performance or a shadow play.

For those with more time and some curiosity about the music-making process, attending a rehearsal is the best way to get an insider's view. Here there is opportunity to sit close to the musicians, hear passages repeated (which clarifies one's perception of them), and feel the physical power of the music at close range. Practices, like ceremonies, are always taking place somewhere, but it may require a bit of sleuthing to find out about them. A casual drive through back roads after dark will often lead to an illuminated balai banjar filled with musicians and instruments. During April and May Festival Gong rehearsals take place daily; these can be located by dropping by one of the music schools and asking in the faculty offices. During morning class hours, the conservatories themselves provide an excellent venue for visitors to hear and see musicians practicing. Many of the faculty speak English and all are available year round to advise people seeking out good music. ISI is located on Jalan Nusa Indah in Denpasar and KOKAR/SMKI is in Batubulan village.

If there is a particular type of music or a specific gamelan group that you wish to hear (such as one of the famous ones mentioned in Chapter Six), it is not at all impractical to commission a command performance by going to the ensemble's village and negotiating directly (perhaps with the help of an interpreter) with the *ketua sekaha gong* (head of the gamelan group). Arrangements can be made to accommodate visitors right in the village at the *banjar* hall or any other suitable space nearby. The price of such a performance will vary according to its length and elaborateness, so it is important to establish scope and cost fairly and firmly beforehand. In any case a group of 10 or so commissioners should find it affordable to hire a troupe of musicians and dancers for an evening's entertainment. Person-to-person contacts between outsiders and village artists of this sort can be very rewarding for both parties, and are likely to result in a memorable event.

A final important venue for hearing music in Bali that bears mention is the yearly Bali Arts Festival, held at the Denpasar Art Center from mid-June to mid-July. An effort is made here to present a diverse selection of classical and modern dance and music at the daily performances. On weekends, thousands of spectators cram into the Ardha Chandra open theater to witness theatrical productions, *gong kebyar* performances, or *sendratari* extravaganzas produced exclusively for the Festival by the conservatories and regional arts councils. Other events at the Festival range from craft exhibits to speech-making contests to academic seminars to fashion shows. Over the years there has also been a steady increase in the presentation of other Indonesian and international art forms.

Learning Balinese Music
Any hands-on opportunity to play Balinese musical instruments can provide insight into the music not obtainable through passive listening. With this kind of direct interaction one learns not just the melodies, *kotekan* and instrumental techniques, but also undergoes the rote learning process, which illuminates the special teacher-student relationship and its implications for the larger role of music in Balinese life. Even just a few lessons will shed light on some of these issues. Lack of musical background or any imagined shortage of aptitude should not be thought of as obstacles, because the Balinese way of learning music involves the development of a different set of perceptive faculties than those that Western music education ordinarily stimulates, and many foreigners—even those without musical experience—find themselves naturally suited to it.

Finding a teacher is a simple matter. By speaking to musicians after a performance, inquiring around the area where you are staying, or by making an excursion to one of the conservatory and asking the advice of faculty members, plenty of suggestions are bound to emerge. Determine first, or ask advice on, what style of music you wish to study. The most frequent choices are gong kebyar, *gender wayang*, and *tingklik* (*gamelan joged bumbung*). If gong kebyar is chosen, begin by learning the mallet and damping

To the Balinese who perform it, gamelan's connection to religion remains its most salient feature.

technique for the *gangsa*, as the main melody and the kotekan parts can both be played on it. It is less productive to begin with other instruments like the *reyong* or *kendang*; grasping their more abstract parts will be much easier once the melodies have been internalized. Lessons can take place at a balai banjar, private home, or other rehearsal space where there are a pair of instruments that can be set up facing each other. Bring a recording device if possible to record the material presented at the lesson for reference and practice later.

Determining appropriate payment for lessons is often a bit tricky because Balinese generally do not teach music privately. Rather all of their instruction is given in a group context and involves long term obligations that are rarely stated explicitly. At the first lesson, make some inquiries. Some teachers with experience teaching foreigners may well have established a set fee, but others will be reluctant to discuss it at all or insist that the amount of payment is entirely dependent upon the student's resources. Don't press the issue, even though it may seem unusual to engage a teacher without a prior understanding about money. Continue studying and ask other foreign students or Balinese musicians about the going rate. Hand the appropriate amount to your teacher, sealed in an envelope, at the end of your study, or, if you will be staying for some time, at intervals during it.

In longer-term situations, it is also worthwhile to consider helping your teacher with some specific need, such as contributing to the cost of home improvements. The total amount of money involved may be equivalent to what a cash payment would be, but the effect is enhanced in that such material purchases simultaneously fulfill a practical purpose and imbue your relationship with your teacher with a sense of family that is inimitably Balinese.

Students with even more ambitious aspirations can enquire at the conservatories about long-term stay permits, academic sponsorship, scholarships, and degree programs. Serious students are advised to cultivate connections with teachers at one of the government music schools. Modest Indonesian government fellowships are available competitively through the Darmasiswa program (darmasiswa.diknas.go.id).

Balinese Music Abroad

A noteworthy component of the expanding interface between Bali and the rest of the world has been the appearance of a number of ensembles based in foreign countries that are devoted to the study, cultivation, and performance of Balinese gamelan on authentic instruments. Some of these groups are based at Indonesian consulates or embassies, others are at universities as part of ethnomusicology curriculums, and a small but growing number are privately owned and maintained. Most cultivate a community membership and model their organization on that of the Balinese banjar and sekaha system. These groups, along with other ones dedicating themselves to Javanese gamelan or to one of the many hybrid Western-made gamelan instruments and styles that have emerged in tandem with the growth of traditional gamelan in the West, have each played their part in raising the music's international profile.

The first Balinese gamelan to be shipped out of Indonesia for study purposes was purchased by the University of California at Los Angeles Music Department in the late 1950s, just before Colin McPhee joined the faculty there. At the time, it was considered unorthodox for students to learn about the music of another culture by actually playing its instruments. But the idea—termed "bimusicality" by ethnomusicologist Mantle Hood—caught on fast. A few years later in Indonesia, the conservatories were established, and there began a regular flow of faculty musicians and dancers going abroad to pursue advanced degrees. Thus the apparatus was in place, outside of Bali, for the formation of student ensembles directed by native masters. This has since been the model followed, whenever possible, by international gamelan groups.

Now there are hundreds of Balinese, Javanese and newly created gamelan groups of all kinds scattered worldwide. Wikipedia's List of Gamelan Ensembles page and http://www.gamelan.org/ (the American Gamelan Institute) plus related links list most active non-Indonesian groups and can give an idea of the concentration of international activity in this field. Indonesian-sponsored Balinese gamelan in the U.S. and Canada are situated at the embassy in Washington D.C. and at the consulates in New York and Los Angeles; a partial list of the universities that maintain them includes UCLA, California Institute of the Arts, Bowling Green State University, Brown University, Florida State University, and the University of British Columbia. Among the community groups are the Sekar Jaya of Oakland, California, and the Galak Tika of Cambridge, Massachusetts, New York (both *gamelan gong kebyar*), and a gamelan angklung in Denver, Colorado. There are active Balinese gamelan in Montreal, Canada; Belfast, Northern Ireland; London, England; Melbourne, Australia; Tokyo, Japan, and more. These ensembles often have busy performance schedules that feature collaborative work with guest Balinese artists. Nearly all of them, including the consular and university groups, are often on the lookout for enthusiastic new players. Information about existing or newly formed gamelan groups can be had by contacting education and culture representatives at Indonesian consulates, or simply by searching the web.

The American Sekar Jaya and the Japanese Sekar Jepun gamelan groups accepted official invitations to participate in the Bali Arts Festival in 1985 and 1987 respectively, thus becoming the first foreign ensembles to formally perform Balinese music and dance in Bali for the Balinese. Sekar Jaya undertook an extensive tour which included performances around the island in competition style with local groups, broadcasts on national television, and a concert in Java. A film of the tour, Kembali, was widely broadcast in North America. Both they and Sekar Jepun were received with great warmth and graciousness by the public, with a tacit acknowledgment that even though neither's presentation was yet at a level with the Balinese, something of a serious beginning had been made in setting standards for the international cultivation of Balinese performing arts. Sekar Jaya returned to Bali regularly between then and 2010 to present programs of experimental as well as traditional works, all well-received and making the group's name synonymous with the idea of foreigners learning to play gamelan. Performance standards for such groups have improved markedly over the years. While Sekar Jaya was admired for its innovation and dedication in 1985, a quarter-century later in 2010 New York's Gamelan Dharma Swara impressed with the strength, precision, and discipline of their musicians and dancers.

Balinese music has leapt in a short time from the isolation to which it was recently confined to the tumultuous musical arenas of our age. And it would seem that the current interaction with foreigners has also reaped some benefits. Some of these are financial, others take less concrete but no less valuable forms and are measured in education, exchange of ideas, recognition, and appreciation. To be sure, the rapidity of change in Bali has had its traumatic effects. A few older styles of music do not hold much interest for today's audiences, and some young Balinese clearly prefer Indonesian and Western pop to anything they hear in the temple. But this is neither a phenomenon that is restricted to Bali nor a potential threat to traditional music in its ongoing ritual role. The continued relevance of gamelan in the daily life of the Balinese, together with the successful export of Balinese musical practice to the rest of the world, make a compelling case for the continued vitality of the tradition.

Oleg Tambulilingan, a dance created in the 1950s, performed with *gamelan gong kebyar*.

Gamelan gong kebyar, Pengosekan village

Gambuh suling (bamboo flutes) and *rebab*, Batuan village.

Suling kantil (small *suling*) are both sweet and shrill and can cut through the loudest gamelan sonorities.

A gamelan foundry at the ancestral home of Pandé Madé Gableran, Blahbatuh village.

Gamelan pelegongan in Teges Kanginan.

7-tone *semar pegulingan* at Banjar Pagan Kelod, Denpasar.

Gamelan gambang, a sacred ensemble, playing at a cremation in Ubud.

Gamelan luang, a rare and sacred type of gamelan maintained in Singapadu village.

4-keyed *gangsa* in the *gamelan angklung*, Mas.

Dalang Nartha with *gender wayang* musicians from Sukawati.
I Wayan Loceng is at Nartha's rear-left.

Jegogan carry the melody in *gamelan angklung*.

Tingklik in gamelan *joged bumbung*,
Singapadu village.

Giant *saron* (or *gangsa jongkok*) in the *gamelan gong gdé*.

The famous *gamelan gambang* from Asak village performs at a variety of ritual occasions.

Young musicians learn social skills and concentration by mastering gamelan techniques.

A festive *gamelan jegog* ensemble from Tegalcangkering village in West Bali.

Iron-keyed *gamelan selunding* (Bugbug village).

CHAPTER TEN

Balinese Music
Since 1990

Visitors to Bali or the island's casual observers may find their appreciation
restricted to what is packaged and marketed to them as a constructed image
of the place. It is all too easy to end up shielded from a fuller view—that is
to say, warts and all—which would bring more appreciation of what a feat
it is for such a small part of such a big country to control its own destiny in
our complex world. This is not to suggest that the Balinese are literally unified in their aspirations, or are able to steer their destiny nearly as much as
they would like. Balinese culture is complex and often self-contradictory,
and consists of much more than the older traditions fueling the island's
renown.

Many forces exert themselves: the Indonesian state, local government,
tourism management, the internet, and the exploitation of land by foreign
investors. There are major issues confronting the upkeep of the environment
and agricultural production, infrastructure, education, and public health.
State and local corruption and lack of accountability persist. Internal migra-
tion of non-Balinese from elsewhere in Indonesia generates ethnic tension.
Confronting these challenges can inspire cooperation but may generate fac-
tions and conflict. Some difficulties are imposed at the national level and
some are regional issues within Bali. One rightly wonders if Bali's destiny
is in too many hands.

Real as they are, for Balinese practicing Agama Hindu Dharma these competing forces still must yield to the hyper-real unseen world and the ancient network of rituals, beliefs and social practices they depend upon to regulate it. That deeper reality is unquestioned, and from it the traditional arts grow like a strong limb. However much the economy may be tossed by faraway trends, and however hard it is to make a decent living—hardships that might fray any culture—the Balinese on the whole try to stay intact, united in their faith in the ultimate authority of what lies behind the surface of the material world. Only a tiny percentage convert or intermarry, and few leave unless they must in order to work. Consequently there is little Balinese diaspora, and the island retains its allure for its own people.

Back in that material world, the past two decades have been a rough ride. In May 1998 president Suharto's bloated New Order government, in power since 1965, was finally brought to its knees in a lethal revolution of riots and protests. The worst of this took place elsewhere in Indonesia, but in North Bali—because the region is poor, neglected, and nursed resentment toward the central government—there were violent protests, arson, and looting. In the more cosmopolitan and tourist-oriented South, reaction was more subdued on the surface, ostensibly because it is generally wealthier than the north and would have risked devastating economic consequences had political unrest discouraged tourism. Devastation arrived nonetheless. An Asian economic crisis and political instability devalued the rupiah to a level from which it has yet to really recover. Inflation soared, and with it the cost of essential goods like rice and gasoline.

October 2002 brought the savage massacre and bombing at the Sari Club in Kuta by Indonesian terrorists. That plus the SARS epidemic of 2003 (deadly, though actually not in Bali) comprised a one-two punch that brought the island to a crawl economically. Visitors virtually stopped coming as Indonesia was placed on travel watch-lists the world over. Homelessness and hunger increased. This exposed the level of dependence on tourism once and for all, as if there were any doubters. The 2004 Indian Ocean tsunami spared Bali but devastated other parts of Indonesia, yet just when things were beginning to recover, more deadly bombs exploded in 2005.

Bali's responses to these tumultuous times have been as multiple as any place's would be, though particularly intense because the island is so small and concentrated, and specifically because of the shock effect and aftermaths of the terror attacks. The initial local response to this was not only to minister bravely to those affected, but also to carry out vast purifications, marshalling any and all spiritual powers to aid healing. The world watched. Enormous ceremonies were held in moving displays of cultural determination. The widely respected former chief of police, Mangku Pastika, who was successful in bringing the bombers to trial, became governor in 2008. It has worked. In 2010, despite worldwide recession, Bali is respectably crowded with visitors.

More broadly, and possibly disturbingly, as Bali's religious and social practices have slowly changed with the times, to some they show symptoms of a certain angst. In recent world history being cosmopolitan and connected has often signaled greater potential to thrive. In Bali this is reflected in the fact that some poor and off-the-beaten-track villages have seen populations and traditions decline. In others more central, wealthy, and wired to the world, cultural and religious vitality has redoubled, in defiance of homogenizing globalization.[1] On the other hand, what if the vitality is partly an outward manifestation of anxiety about Bali's fate, rather than an inner spiritual confidence? Behind the pageantry, does outlaying ever-more resources for lavish rituals (and sometimes subcontracting the making of offerings) conceal the chronic modern maladies of stress and uncertainty? Even as digitally wired young Balinese enact rituals, are they growing paradoxically more alienated from local communities? At these interfaces preserving *kebalian*—Balineseness—seems to be on everyone's mind, not to mention officially promoted in the media. Some see it as grassroots empowerment. Others think it is just the conventional powers promoting conformity, hardly a change from the Suharto days. Still others see the growth of individualism as pernicious, and the new religious extravagance one of the only tools they have to resist it. But all agree that the culture must live, and no one can deny that thus far it has.

Throughout, *gamelan* music remains vital, and has been on the move quickly and dramatically. This is especially remarkable since, unlike, say, African traditional music, it has inspired few commercially viable international crossovers, and doesn't seem to be cut out for more than a tiny niche in the transnational pop music scene. Yet right at home the past twenty

---

1 Confident awareness of this was summed up with the t-short slogan gloBALIzation, popular around 2003.

years saw exciting developments in preservation of older genres and innovation of new ones, plus new layers of music's social aspects. We have to
understand the latter before speaking of the other two.

Social changes in Balinese Music, 1990–2010

Most if not all the secular innovations in gamelan music initiated in the
final decades of the last century continue apace. The Bali Arts Festival
(PKB), now over thirty years old, is still held every June and July, augmented by regional festivals such as the one in Ubud, begun in 2006. The
annual Festival Gong also continues strongly, although in some years it has
been reconfigured as a showcase rather than a competition. The singing
of poetry has enjoyed widespread new popularity, and is celebrated yearly
with the Dharma Gita festival. Women's gamelan no longer raise eyebrows,
and festivals of teenage and children's gamelan take place regularly. Only
once—in 2001—were mixed *gender* gamelan mandated by the organizers
for the Festival Gong, a controversial move that was grudgingly acceded to
for that year but did not stick. Looking ahead to 2015, people are already
talking excitedly about a major international festival to celebrate the designated centenary of *gamelan gong kebyar*.

While older contexts for music—village, temple, *banjar* and school—are
still robust, the *sanggar*, which roughly means "community art collective",
has taken on an extremely important role. Sanggar are founded by individuals, families, or friends, rather than as part of traditional or civic law. It
takes entrepreneurial spirit and some capital (to purchase instruments and
dance costumes, for example) to start and manage one, and the fact that this
impetus comes from the private sector in a rising middle class is truly new.
A sanggar's primary purpose is usually to make music and dance for their
own sakes, not to fill a religious or civic need, though virtually all sanggar
are willing and gratified to be asked to contribute to rituals as needed.

Most sanggar are set up in a family compound with a *balai* (a freestanding
traditional building or hall) big enough to install a gamelan in and to use as
a rehearsal/community area. Some set up in commercial spaces, such as the
well-known sanggar Perinting Mas, famous in the '90s, which rehearsed
in a Denpasar printer's workshop after hours. The very first sanggar were
established in the late 1970s in Denpasar as the early generations of conservatory graduates looked for ways to continue playing the kind of expert,

high-quality music they made when they bonded as students. Students can come from anywhere on the island, hence sanggar were also genuinely new in that their members were not tied to a single village or temple, as had previously been the case.

Since sanggar are private they are free to do what they please. Two of the most successful are Sanggar Çudamani of Pengosekan village (www.cudamani.org), founded by Dewa Putu Berata, Dewa Ketut Alit, and their two other brothers, and Sanggar Semara Ratih of banjar Taman, Ubud (www.semararatih.org), founded by Anak Agung Anom Putra. Both have been active since the 1990s. They nurture crack gamelan ensembles and fine dance troupes—arguably the most polished and supple ever known to Bali—not to mention maintain (as noted) web presences and networks of international connections. They apply for grants from philanthropies like the Ford Foundation, tour abroad, offer workshops, residencies, seminars, classes and summer programs (for foreign students), engage older teachers from other parts of Bali, and commission composers and choreographers to create new work—some of it in collaboration with outsiders. Some sanggar sponsor separate ensembles—for women, for children, for teenagers—to keep the flame of gamelan kindled in the local area.

The proliferation of sanggar doesn't weaken tradition, but reconfigures its demography and loyalties. And it reflects the times. People are more mobile now, and think of art as an enterprise *as well as* a religious and community service. Yet the inspiration and ideology behind sanggar is to preserve, in a new way, the ethos of the banjar. Sanggar are seen as a partial refuge from the pressures of modern life, a place where friends—linked together by life experience or interests rather than banjar affiliation—can unite to safeguard tradition. Village and banjar ensembles play on, but somewhat less dependably. Sanggar are where the action is.

Unquestionably, sanggar have ramped up the standards of Balinese gamelan technique and performance. In the most successful, the membership sustains close personal ties. Members are usually young, and just out of school. They play, eat, and even sleep near their instruments, participate and assist in each others' daily lives and work, and can develop preternatural communal rapport. Too, most sanggar players now are formally educated and musically self-aware. To see a good sanggar group learn a new composition together can defy credulity, as they memorize and master in minutes long complex passages that their parents' generation might have struggled with for days, or even given up on. Yet they themselves can be conflicted, lamenting that their virtuosity is too light and easy for their own good. Some say they cannot attain the gravity and effort that makes their predecessors' music—hearkening from the era when musicians were unschooled, barefoot rice farmers without cell phones or internet connections—an object of melancholy nostalgia. Aurally, there is no way to miss the difference. To juxtapose the virtuosity of Çudamani or Semara Ratih with that of the 1970s Perean group (Chapter Six) is to contrast consummate professionalism with unselfconscious, naïve music-making. The latter suggests to young musicians today that there has been a fall from grace, a notion felt as a pang with every text message sent during rehearsal.

Along with the individual initiative fueling the growth of sanggar, individual musicians have risen to the fore as composers and leaders more than ever, especially as a result of international attention. Senior composer Nyoman Windha, whose music of the '80s was described at the beginning of Chapter Seven, has gone on to an extraordinary career. He composes in Bali for the gamelan festivals and other occasions, for the Indonesian government for national holidays or other spectacles, and for gamelan groups internationally. He taught in the U.S. and Europe many times between 1989 and 2005, and in 2004 completed a graduate degree in music composition at Mills College in California. He now creates extravagant, ambitious, and culturally referential musical fusions, like the 2006 Mulih ke Bali (Come Home to Bali), a mix of instruments and styles from Western and Indonesian music, with a band of players from the U.S., England, Japan and all over Indonesia. Behind the musicians, Windha screened archive footage from the 1920s and '30s depicting pristine Balinese beaches, forests, and wildlife, and the simpler life of the day. As for the music, there was some irony in how he used the cosmopolitan practice of fusion and cross-cultural blend to express his concern for Bali's culture and natural environment.

Musical Changes I : Preservation
Knowing the value of preserving and celebrating heritage is an important legacy of the twentieth century that has generated research, education, and cultural awareness all over the world. In Bali, one result has been that many of the older musical traditions described in the foregoing chapters, similar

to traditions everywhere, have acquired more of a museum-like or historical quality. The conservatory built a gamelan museum on campus housing
all kinds of instruments. Some preservationism is abetted by research and
publication. The grassroots revivals of certain vocal genres (like the recita-
tion of *kakawin* poetry) were partly inspired by the appearance of instruc-
tional primers that make the practice more accessible.

Rare and sacred gamelan are still practiced in the few places they were
before but tend to strike people as something belonging to the past. Ensembles of those types used to be defined by a certain traditional context—say
a specific ceremony or village—but have been singled out by government
education and arts ministries for preservation. Such a tradition might become the subject of scholarly investigation and get taught in schools. An
interested patron (Balinese or foreign) might even order a set of instruments
and cultivate it themselves. In some cases repertoires have been painstakingly reconstructed, which was the case for the extraordinary project of
reviving the music, dance, and theater of the *gamelan gambuh* in Batuan
village in the 1990s, steered by the formidable Italian scholar and dancer
Cristina Formaggia (1946–2008), or the patient efforts of elder musician
Wayan Sinti and his sanggar Manikasanti to revive the sacred *gamelan
gambang*'s repertoire of accompanied songs, which were long taken to be
extinct. Unlike many places in Indonesia and elsewhere, we are fortunate
that no Balinese musical genre has died of late.

To take another example, the ritual *gamelan gong gdé* lives on in a scant
few mountain villages like Sulahaan and Batur that have been its bastion.
But musicians' average ages there are now much higher than they were.
Many have died and not been replaced as young people leave for bigger
towns, or opt not to learn the staid old repertoire because it is so un-*kebyar*-
like: abstract, long, and only played at certain rituals. Meanwhile *gong gdé*
was introduced and learned at the conservatory in the '90s. Although its
traditional contexts exert a weaker hold than they did, its musical style became second nature to a generation of young musicians, more educated and
professional than their elders. They then went on to compose new music
referencing it, in some cases kebyar-izing it by upping the tempo and adding modern-style musical elaborations. In Batubulan village an energetic
musician named Ketut Suanda was able to afford his own gong gdé instruments to use in his sanggar Cendana, to make new kinds of music and

drama. One can contrast the sense of "past" for people viewing Batur and Sulahaan as outsiders, with the emerging sense of gong gdé as a living part of a shared musical vocabulary that can be exploited for present and future music. In the twenty-first century music can leave its old village and ritual homes to live on in new ones, changing sometimes radically in new combinations and adaptations.

Musical Changes II : Experimentation, and All Kinds of New Music
Indeed for nearly all ambitious musicians in Bali these days it is virtually a requirement to compose, create, knowingly extend, and in some cases try to break with tradition. *Musik kontemporer* is the umbrella term for this genre of mainly one-off musical experiments. In traditional village and banjar contexts gamelan players were passive recipients of what they were taught and expected to play. Now most dedicated musicians age 40 and under have gone to the conservatory, and composed a major work as a thesis project. Conservatory graduation became a forum for musical avant-gardisms and fusions, especially when bolder students tried to test the ideology of their teachers. Such musicians have listened to music from all over the world, and met many foreign musicians either in Bali or through their own travels. They may use new instruments or adapt outside musical ideas. They may chafe at authority or perceive their education system as demoralized or ineffective, and express that anger in their music. They mix instruments from different gamelan, or rejigger them, or play them with unconventional techniques. Sometimes they arouse the indignation of their teachers and evaluating juries. But even the most radical voices in new Balinese music actually profess reverence for tradition—it is the perceived narrow definitions of tradition imposed by the strictures of formal education, state corruption, or the pressures of modern life that they are reacting against.

Here is musicologist Andrew McGraw's surprising description of one such recent *kontemporer* "event":

> For his 2006 final recital at ISI Bali [the conservatory], the young composer Sang Nyoman Arsawijaya (Sauman) created a radically experimental work, entitled "Grausch", for a small ensemble of five musicians performing four sets of cut but untuned telephone poles, a set of detuned gamelan keys amplified and distorted using guitar pedals (performed by hacking at them with small handsaws) various bits of *rebab* and a gong. The cacophony culminates in Sauman's "playing" the

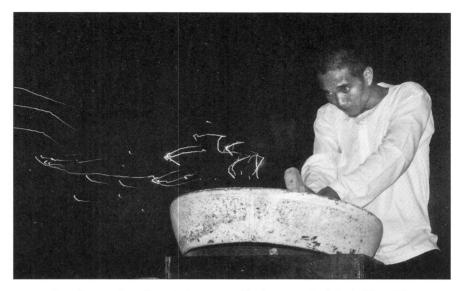

Sang Nyoman Arsawijaya playing a gong with a hammer and grinder in "Grausch".
Photo: family of Sang Nyoman Arsawijaya.

gong with a hammer in one hand and an electric grinder in the other. Several members of the ISI jury arrived at the performance wearing (and distributing) earplugs, a comical reaction by musicians who regularly play some of the loudest acoustic music in the world. A section of the audience walked out...In Balinese traditional contexts the gong is a revered symbol of one's ancestors, elders or teachers; it is an abode of spirits and is given special offerings and prayers. Sauman's intention was not only to explore new sound qualities and shock audiences, but to make a provocative statement of protest against the ISI faculty who, according to him, did not fulfill their roles as thoughtful, open-minded composers, mentors or teachers. By torching the gong Sauman was, essentially, flaming the faculty (2009:131–2).

Of course that is an extreme case. Sauman is no charlatan; he now serves the musical community as head of a vital young composers' sanggar in Denpasar, P.D. Parkir.

It is sometimes said that music can predict the future, and that when radical change comes to music, broader social changes will follow. Perhaps this is because unbeknownst even to themselves, musicians give voice to mounting social pressures nonverbally, through the feelings and symbols evoked by the music they make. Whether or not that is the case, in 1995, three years before the riots of 1998, the bottom dropped out of new music in Bali. Gdé Yudane, a single-mindedly nonconformist composer from banjar Kaliungu in Denpasar, introduced his Lebur Seketi (roughly, "broken melodies") in the Festival Gong, in which he intentionally scrambled or reversed all the familiar elements and conventions of kebyar style. For him they had become ossified and so this was a musical urge, not an overt political statement. And unlike the specialized musik kontemporer, this was music for the broad public. He was derided at first, but that composition plus others in the following years opened the floodgates. By now the conventions of kebyar are just one choice among many for the next generation. One example is the gifted Wayan Sudirana of Ubud (born 1980), who profited from chances to study African, Indian and Korean drumming traditions seriously, as well as learn European harmony. His music draws extensively on all of those things; what is equally remarkable is how smoothly musicians in their teens and twenties are able to absorb them. Sudirana's composition Arakok (2006), for partial *gamelan semaradana* (see below) with trumpet and saxophone, is excerpted on track 12 of the book CD; his other innovative works include Navadaza (2010).

The complexity and unfamiliarity of new musical materials has also fostered composers' use of musical notation (the Balinese kind) to set down their ideas. This allows them to be more sure of what they are imagining and teaching, though they still transmit the music orally to the players, who memorize as they always have. The new complexity has made rich new rhythmic and melodic techniques unknown in earlier eras second nature to today's players. With a little perspective it will likely become clear that these recent changes are as formative as those that gave birth to the kebyar style a century ago. Other well-known composers now include Madé Arnawa, Desak Madé Laksmi, Madé Subandi, and many others.

International exchanges and cross-cultural collaborations have strongly marked the times. The South Indian dance company Ragamala, based in Minnesota, U.S.A., did a collaborative work with sanggar Çudamani adapted from the Hindu Ramayana saga, and performed it in both places. American composer Evan Ziporyn wrote an opera based on Colin McPhee's memoir *A House in Bali*, for the combined forces of a gamelan led by Dewa Ketut Alit and the well-known Bang On a Can contemporary music ensemble of New York. It was premiered in Ubud in 2009 and went on to major performances in Berkeley, Boston, and New York.

Experimentation can mean that music not sounding at all Balinese in any traditional sense has sometimes been presented as if it were. There is nothing wrong with that—cultures shouldn't be straightjackets. But it raises the question: if a Balinese is making it, is it then Balinese music? In that case, we should embrace the many international styles of popular music that have grassroots adherents in Bali. Death metal, punk, reggae, and rap are all made here copiously, and Balinese groups like Superman is Dead and Phobia are widely known through MTV Asia, YouTube, and their concert tours. Balawan, a gifted rock and jazz guitarist from Batuan village, crosses back over, bringing gamelan elements into much of his electric pop.

Back in the Mainstream: Gamelan Semaradana

Twentieth century Balinese music was dominated by the gong kebyar, described in Chapter Six. But around 1986, the gamelan semaradana was invented at the Denpasar workshop of senior composer and gamelan tuner Wayan Beratha. It filled a perceived need to be able to do more musically with a single set of instruments, instead of having each genre restricted to the ensemble in which it was cultivated separately over the centuries. The significance of the new ensemble's name is disputed. *Semara* means love, or refers to the god of love in Hindu mythology; and *dana* means fire (as in sacrificial fire) which in turn suggests giving or self-sacrifice. There is a classical kakawin poem describing Semara's immolation by the god Siwa after waking him from meditation. Fire for casting bronze, and the idea of love or sacrifice for music are appropriately ancient and inspiring metaphors for the new gamelan.

Semaradana is just like gong kebyar in instrumentation and it looks much the same, with the major difference that extra keys and gongs have been inserted among the others so the instruments are a bit longer. For instance, the *pemadé* and *kantilan* have twelve keys each instead of ten. Overall, this transforms them from the five-tone *pélog* mode used in kebyar to the full seven-tone scale used in earlier gamelan like *gambuh, semar pegulingan, luang, selunding*, and *gambang* (see Chapter Four). The extra two tones do not simply fill in gaps between certain tones of kebyar instruments, but do so in a way that gives each of the numerous different five-tone modes extractable from it a distinct character. Semaradana musicians can thus play repertoire from all of these older ensembles (and more) *plus* that of kebyar, on the same sort of expanded, versatile instruments used in kebyar itself. This led to new arrangements of older music, and gave musicians a chance to master several repertoires while staying put in a single ensemble. Meanwhile the kebyar style can be played equally well on the same gamelan. Thus even with the gradual rise of semaradana in the years since it was introduced, kebyar repertoire remains alive, intact and accessible to the audiences who love it.

By about 1990 less than five semaradana had been made but twenty years on there are more than 150. Though not a radical or experimental break in the tradition—in fact its creation was really something of a traditionalist move—semaradana nonetheless opened many unexpected doors. With it, younger composers such as the ones mentioned earlier rediscovered the potential of the different musical worlds suggested by the seven-tone scale and combined them in ways that had never been heard before. They infused them with kebyar's dynamism, rhythmic complexity, and virtuosity, and have been coming up with a whole new vocabulary for gamelan music.

Kebyar instrument sets—of which there are at least 1600—are clearly still far more common, but semaradana is hands down the new standard bearer for modern Balinese gamelan, the new mainstream of the tradition. Many sanggar have them, and they are in standard use at the conservatory. Several have been shipped to gamelan groups in Great Britain, Canada, Singapore, and the United States.

Postlude: August 16, 2010

Today I pay a long-awaited visit to Wayan Suweca, the kebyar drummer we met briefly in Chapter Six, at his home in Oongan, a Denpasar suburb. He is a favorite friend and teacher with whom I partnered on the drums during the early years of Gamelan Sekar Jaya in California, and it has been far too long since we really talked. Suweca was that group's first leader and inspired many of us for life. But for most of the past thirty years he has stayed close to home, fulfilling modest duties as a teacher at the conservatory, and performing when asked.

Suweca is an unsurpassed wizard of the drum whose electrifying stage presence and piercing eye contact can ignite a blaze. But unlike some of his peers, he was never a modernist creative firebrand jostling to compose daring music for high-profile festivals and tours. Rather he was a reverent culture-bearer humbled by the achievements of his ancestors and obsessed with mastering them. Seated in his front room, we revisit a much-loved

I Wayan Suweca

thread: praising great Balinese musicians of the past we have known. He vocalizes favorite drum patterns learned from them, sounding like a "fugitive morse code" (a metaphor Colin McPhee once used), eyes wide and smiling, reflexively moving his hands as if playing. He recites the litany of drummers of yesteryear whose personal hallmarks these rhythms were, marshalling and channeling them as though they are his best and oldest friends. Which they are.

We marvel at twentieth century masters like Manik, Mandera, Beratha, Regog, Griya, Pogog, Sibang, Kuna, Kalé, Senken, of course his father Konolan—the list goes on and on. "Manik taught me how to make three different kinds of *pak* sound on the left side skin, and Beratha had so many *dag* right hand variations—but he never overused them. Mandera taught me that posture and style are as important as technique. He said 'use your hands to dance. Raise them up, spread your fingers, and make them alive. Follow your hands with your eyes as they return to the drum. No one will be able to take their eyes off you, and you will have power and command.'" He demonstrates, and it is truer than ever.

Perhaps as a consequence of Suweca's singular devotion to the past, the Balinese limelight of musical trends has sometimes favored others. But where he once evinced some bitterness and self-doubt in response, there is now maturity and satisfaction. At age 62, he is quieter, having grown into the role of an elder musician, as his father taught him it is indeed meant to be. Suweca told me ages ago: "My dad said a young musician plays kebyar. It is fire and energy, tight friendships and excitement, bravado, charisma, flash, and pride. An older one turns inward, recites kakawin, and plays more spiritual music like *lelambatan* or *gender wayang*, reflective music that has no bottom to its meaning and significance. There is a time in life for everything."

So Suweca has put away youthful things. In 2007 he went back to school for the graduate degree of Magister at Indonesian Hindu University (UNHI) in Denpasar, and is finishing a thesis on the spiritual and religious significance of the *gamelan gender wayang*. (Suweca learned this tradition from his father too, and is as good a gender player as he is a drummer. This is a whole other, equally deep aspect of his musicianship.). He has one grandchild and three grown children, all serious musicians—even and especially his daughter Putu, the eldest, who graduated *cum laude* from the conservatory. But this is not surprising, as it was Konolan who thought nothing of teaching both of Suweca's sisters music decades ago, before other women played at all. One sister, Suryatini, was half of the first pair of female conservatory graduates (see Chapter Seven), and has had a significant musical career in Bali and abroad. No doubt it never occurred to the modest Konolan that he was radicalizing Balinese music. He was too engrossed with his art to do otherwise, and anyway not the type.

In the next room Suweca's wife Ketut, their children, plus in-laws, cousins, nephews, and nieces, loll on a big bamboo mat watching Japanese *manga* on the widescreen TV, sniffing lunch in the air. It is a normal Sunday with lots of people around, coming and going. Two of the youngest kids are playing with shadow puppets, imagining that they are puppeteers, and one of the cousins is listening to gamelan on an iPod. There is a mass-produced aluminum frame sofa, as well as an imposing hardwood dining room set, every last cranny of which is carved in flowery Balinese motifs. Mallets and small gongs are strewn about. Balinese paintings of mythological scenes and photos of Suweca performing adorn the walls. It's hot, and a ceiling fan turns.

After our meal we go in the back and enter a larger room, open to the outside at one end: Suweca's gamelan workshop. He has had a side business tuning and selling instruments for years. Here are a full gamelan gong kebyar, two sets of gamelan gender wayang, a *gamelan angklung*, a cabinet full of drums, and all sorts of other instruments scattered around. Gesturing to the kebyar, Suweca explains that he "had these instruments made to combine my two favorite village gamelan in Bali: the carving and design of Peliatan's, and the tuning of Sadmerta's." They are sparkling.

"What are you planning for them?" I ask.

"These aren't for selling. I've been getting some friends together to play lelambatan. Not from the banjar, though. That has gotten too hard. Everyone's schedules are too full. This is just old friends from around south Bali, people I've played with over the years, who I know will make the time. You know, just before my dad died, he made a special request of me: play *tabuh kutus* [*tabuh 8*—see Chapter Four] whenever you can."

"Those are the longest lelambatan. It's rare to hear them."

"Right, one time through the *pengawak* melody alone can take about six minutes. There is amazing spiritual power in that music. When you play it you are in a dream, transported somewhere beautiful. Only old people know those pieces now. And even then the only ones one ever hears are Pelayon and Lasem. Have you ever heard another? No. But my dad had one, Kartika, which he taught me. Probably he learned it from the musicians who used to play in the *puri badung* [nobles' residence] before Independence. I'm constantly singing it in my head, practicing the *trompong* part. [*He sings a phrase.*] We're going to do those, plus other temple music, and when we're ready we'll play them at ceremonies whenever we can, just around here. We're going to use the original drum patterns, the simple and sparse ones—but tricky. It will feel great. It's not about anything else—just serving the community, and keeping that music alive. We can't do differently."

My fingers wander on to the gender wayang keys. One set is shiny new, and the other is well-used, with a deep purple hue in the bronze. The wooden cases are simple, unpainted and uncarved.

"Listen to this." Suweca plays the same note on each of the two larger gender in the old set, once for each of the five tones in the scale, to bring out the shimmering paired tuning. The notes hang in the air like hummingbirds. "I will never sell these instruments either. I last tuned them in 1985 and they are still in total accord. Can you believe it? They are perfect. Each interval different, each matched pair like *lingga* and *yoni*, female and male:

rwa bhineda [the simultaneous unity and duality of opposites in Balinese philosophy]. So deep and rewarding to play."

Then he carefully chooses two sets of mallets, rejecting a few. "Komang, *mai malu! [c'mere!]*", he calls. After a brief moment, his son and third child ambles in, sheepish and a little groggy after the TV. He is handed mallets, and sits, and smiles. No words are exchanged.

They start to play Merak Ngelo, and a few seconds later one of the cousins comes in and joins them. I know the tune well, but every time I hear it played its asymmetrical twists and turns hook me back in. On these magnificent instruments it sounds especially supple and plaintive. The logic, energy, and ingeniousness of the music are so beguiling. The rise and fall of the mallets' interlocking motions keep my eyes busy too, as always. They've chosen a medium tempo and a gentle dynamic. Others would play it a lot louder and faster. A few father-son glances and they make the transitions easily, speeding up just a little before the end.

I have to go soon, but Suweca has more to tell me. He knows I used to worry about him after his stint in America with us, because he seemed to take a long time to feel good in his own skin back in Bali. "Those problems are way behind me. Here is what feels good now: I am back in school, studying the religious significance of art. Everyone in class is less than half my age, but so what? And I have taken care of some important things.

"After my father died my siblings and I pooled resources and rebuilt the *marajaan* [house temple] in our ancestral home. I am the eldest son, and it's especially my obligation to see to that. We tore down one of the other pavilions because no one was using it, also and built a special *balai taksu*, a shrine where we make offerings to the forces maintaining the spiritual and artistic power that generations of my family have been graced with. It just about did us in financially but now I have that secure feeling of meeting my obligations and protecting my ancestors' and my own family's musical lineage. Here's the proof: my children all play well. Now no matter how old I get, I will have someone to play gender with. So my life is just as it should be."

Appendix

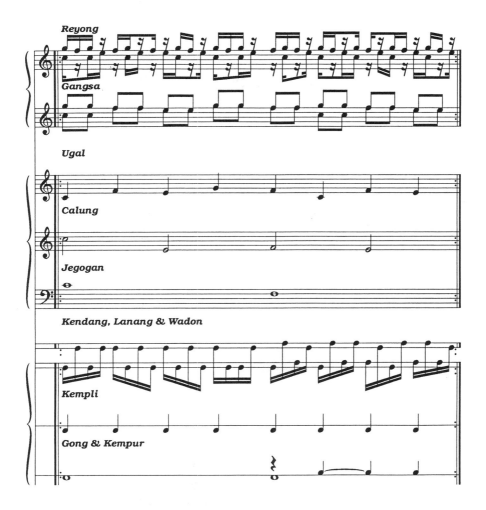

Baris score in standard Western notation.

Further Reading

The published literature on Bali is vast and covers many fields of inquiry—history, anthropology, sociology, economics, religion, agronomy, arts and culture, and so on. A comprehensive bibliography would weigh in at more than a thousand pages. Below I suggest only the most well-known writings focused on music, plus a select few on dance, drama and shadow play. I have included publications in several languages and at various levels of specialization. Basset 1995, Gold 2004 and Dibia/Ballinger 2004, for example, appeal to an audience similar to the one addressed by this book. McPhee 1946 and Coast 1953 are personal memoirs of a sort. Bakan 1999 is oriented toward ethnography, while Tenzer 2000 is an analytical and technical study for musicians and composers. Kunst and van Wely's 1925 monograph has historical interest as the first-ever on the subject, based on a scant week of research.

The dissertation titles give a broader sense of the research being carried out; many of the authors have also published articles. Some more recent ones plan books based on their work. The list of chapters and articles is necessarily limited—the profusion is too great to do justice to here.

Books and Scholarly Monographs since 1925

Bakan, Michael. 1999. *Music of Death and New Creation: Experiences in the World of* Balinese Baleganjur. Chicago: University of Chicago Press.

Bandem, Madé, ed. and trans. 1986. *Prakempa: Sebuah Lontar Gambelan Bali.* Denpasar: Akademi Seni Tari Indonesia.

Bandem, Madé and Fredrik E. DeBoer. 1995 [1981]. *From Kaja to Kelod: Balinese Dance in Transition.* Kuala Lumpur: Oxford University Press.

Basset, Catherine. 1995. *Musiques de Bali à Java: L'Ordre et la Fête.* Paris: Cité de la Musique/Actes Sud.

Coast, John. 1953. Dancing Out of Bali. New York: Putnam.

De Zoete, Beryl, and Walter Spies. 1937. *Dance and Drama in Bali.* London: Faber & Faber.

Dibia, Wayan. 1996. *Kecak: The Vocal Chant of Bali.* Bali: Hartanto Art Books.

Dibia, I Wayan, and Rucina Ballinger. 2004. *Balinese Dance, Drama and Music: A Guide to the Performing Arts of Bali.* Singapore: Periplus Editions.

Formaggia, Cristina (ed.). 2000. *Gambuh, Drama Tari Bali,* (*The Gambuh Preservation Project.*). Jakarta: Yayasan Lontar.

Gold, Lisa. 2004. *Music in Bali: Experiencing Music, Expressing Culture.* New York: Oxford University Press.

Herbst, Edward. 1997. *Voices in Bali: Energies and Perceptions in Vocal Music and Dance Theater.* Hanover: University Press of New England.

Hobart, Angela. 1987. *Dancing Shadows of Bali.* London: Taylor and Francis.

Illing, Kai-Torsten. 1990. *Das Joged Bumbung: Unterhaltungsmusik und-tanze auf Bali.* Teil I-II. Hamburg: Karl Dieter Wagner Verlag der Musikalienhandlung

Kunst, Jaap, and C.J.A. Kunst-van Wely. 1925. *De Toonkunst van Bali.* Weltevreden, Koninklijk Bataviaasch Genootschaap.

Mack, Dieter. 2003. *Bali, Länderheft der Reihe, Musik der Welt.* Oldershausen: Lugert Verlag.

McPhee, Colin. 1966. *Music in Bali: A Study in Form and Instrumental Organization in Balinese Orchestral Music.* New Haven: Yale University Press.

McPhee, Colin.1946. *A House in Bali.* New York: The John Day Company.

Oja, Carol. 1990. *Colin McPhee: A Composer in Two Worlds.* Washington, D.C.: Smithsonian Press.

Rembang, Nyoman. 1984/5. *Hasil Pendokumentasian Notasi Gending-Gending Lelambatan Klasik Pegongan Daerah Bali.* Denpasar: Departemen Pendidikan.

Schaareman, Danker, ed., *Balinese Music in Context: A Sixty-Fifth Birthday Tribute to Hans Oesch.* Winterthur: Amadeus Verlag, Forum Ethnomusicologicum 4.

Schlager, Ernst. 1976. *Rituelle Siebenton-Musik Auf Bali.* Winterthur: Amadeus Verlag, Forum Ethnomusicologicum 1.

Sukerta, Pandé Madé. 2009. *Gong Kebyar Buleleng: Perubahan dan Keberlanjutan Tradisi Gong Kebyar.* Surakarta: ISI Press.

Tenzer, Michael. 2000. *Gamelan Gong Kebyar: the Art of Twentieth-Century Balinese Music*. Chicago: University of Chicago Press.

Toth, Andrew. 1980. 1980. *Recordings of the Traditional Music of Bali and Lombok*. Bloomington: The Society for Ethnomusicology Special Series No. 4.

Vickers, Adrian. 2005. *Journeys of Desire: The Balinese Malat in Text and History*. Leiden; KITLV Series VKI. Zurbuchen, Mary. 1987. *The Language of Balinese Shadow Theater*. Princeton: Princeton University Press.

PhD Dissertations since 1971

Bandem, I Madé. 1980. *Wayang Wong in Contemporary Bali* (Wesleyan University)

Basset, Catherine. 2004. *Tome I: Gong, Vingt Ans de Recherche; Tome II: Musiques de Bali à Java: L'Ordre et la Fête; Tome III: Gamelan, Architecture Sonor (internet site: /www.cite-musique.fr/gamelan/); Tone IV: Roue Sonore, Cosmogonie et Structures Essentielles de L'offrande; Tome V: Bibliographie et Table des Matières*. (Université Paris X-Nanterre, Laboratoire d'Ethnomusicologie UMR 8574)

Dibia, I Wayan. 1992. *Arja: a Sung Dance-Drama of Bali* (UCLA)

Downing, Sonja Lynn. 2008. *Arjuna's Angels: Girls Learning Gamelan Music in Bali*. (University of California, Santa Barbara)

Gold, Lisa. 1998. *The Gender Wayang Repertoire in Theater and Ritual: a Study of Balinese Musical Meaning*. (University of California, Berkeley)

Gray, Nicholas. 1996. *No Tree is Untouched by the Wind: Aspects of Improvisation in Balinese Gender Wayang*. (School of Oriental and African Studies, University of London)

Heimarck, Brita. 1999. *Balinese Discourses on Music: Musical Modernization in the Ideas and Practices of Shadow Play Performers from Sukawati and the Indonesian College of the Arts*. (Cornell University)

McGraw, Andrew Clay. 2005. *Musik Kontemporer: Experimental Music by Balinese Composers*. (Wesleyan University)

Ornstein, Ruby. 1971. *Gamelan Gong Kebjar: the Development of a Balinese Musical Tradition*. (UCLA)

Rai, I Wayan, 1996. *Balinese Gamelan Semar Pegulingan Saih Pitu: the Modal System.* (University of Maryland)

Rubenstein, Raechelle. 1988. *Beyond the Realm of the Senses: the Balinese Ritual of Kakawin Composition.* (University of Sydney)

Sanger, Annette. 1986. *The Role of Music and Dance in the Social and Cultural Life of Two Balinese Villages.* (Queen's University of Belfast)

Vonck, Henrice M. 1997. *Manis and Keras in Image, Word and Music of Wayang Kulit in Tejakula North Bali.* (University of Amsterdam)

Wallis, Richard. 1980. *The Voice as a Mode of Cultural Expression in Bali.* (University of Michigan)

Wakeling, Katharine. 2010. *Representing Balinese Music: A Study of the Practice and Theorization of Balinese Gamelan.* (University of London)

Journal Articles and Book Chapters

Bakan, Michael. 1998. "From Oxymoron to Reality: Agendas of Gender and the Rise of Balinese Women's *Gamelan Beleganjur* in Bali, Indonesia." *Asian Music* 29(1):37–86.

Davies, Stephen. 2008. 'The Origins of Balinese Legong, '*Bijdragen tot de taal-, land- en volkenkund* (BKI), 164 (2/3), 194–211.

DeVale, Sue Carole and Wayan Dibia. 1991. "*Sekar Anyar:* An Exploration of Meaning in Balinese *Gamelan.*" *The World of Music* 33(1): 5–51.

Downing, Sonja Lynn. 2010. "Agency, Leadership and Gender Negotiation in Balinese Girls' Gamelans", *Ethnomusicology* 54/1: 54–80.

Gray, Nicholas. 2010. "Of One Family? Improvisation, Variation and Compositon in Balinese *Gender Wayang*", *Ethnomusicology* 54/2:224–56.

Harnish, David. 2000. "The World of Music Composition in Bali", *Journal of Musicological Research* 20: 1–40.

Hood, Mantle. 1966. "*Slendro* and *Pélog* Redefined," *UCLA Selected Reports*, Vol. 1, 28–48.

Keeler, Ward: "A Musical Journey Through Java and Bali" *(Indonesia Journal,* 1975)

Koichi, M. 1990. "Balinese Mouthharps: Genggong and Ngo", *Koukin Journal*, i: 18–19.

McGraw, A. (2009) "Radical Tradition: Balinese Musik Kontemporer," *Ethnomusicology* 53(1): 115–41.

McGraw, A. 2008. "Different Temporalities: The Time of Balinese Music," Yearbook for Traditional Music 40: 136–62.

McPhee, Colin. 1936. "The Balinese Gender Wayang and its Music", *Djawa* XVl/l. (Reprinted in Belo, Jane, *Traditional Balinese Culture,* Columbia University Press, New York, 1970)

McPhee, Colin. 1936. *Children and Music in Bali, Djawa* XVIII/6. (Reprinted in Belo, Jane, *Traditional Balinese Culture,* Columbia University Press, New York, 1970)

Peterman, Lewis. 1989. "Regional Variations in Balinese Gender Wayang Music: a Comparison and Analysis of Different Local Versions of Gending Rebong", *Progress Reports in Ethnomusicology* 2: 1–16.

Richter, Karl. 1992. *"Slendro-Pélog* and the Conceptualisation of Balinese Music: Remarks on the *Gambuh* Tone System," In Schaareman, D., ed., *Balinese Music in Context: A Sixty-Fifth Birthday Tribute to Hans Oesch.* Winterthur: Amadeus Verlag, Forum Ethnomusicologicum 4. 195–220.

Schaareman, Danker. 1980. "The Gamelan Gambang of Tatulingga, Bali." *Ethnomusicology* 24(3): 465–82

Schumacher, Rudiger. 1992. "Bala Ugu" und "Aji Kembang": zwei balinesische Gesänge zwischen den Gattungen", in *Von der Vielfalt musikalischer Kultur,* ed. R. Schumacher, 465–86.

Tenzer, Michael. 2006. "Oleg Tumulilingan: Layers of Time and Melody in Balinese Music." in *Analytical Studies in World Music*, ed. Michael Tenzer. New York: Oxford University Press, 205–36.

Tenzer, Michael. 2005. "Wayan Gandera and the Hidden History of Gamelan Gong Kebyar" *Asian Music* 36/1: 109–22.

Toth, Andrew.1975. "The *Gamelan Luang* of Tangkas, Bali." *Selected Reports in Ethnomusicology* 2(2):65–79.

Vickers, Adrian. 1992. *"Kidung* Meters and the Interpretation of the *Malat."* In Schaareman, D., ed., *Balinese Music in Context: A Sixty-Fifth Birthday Tribute to Hans Oesch.* Winterthur: Amadeus Verlag,

Forum Ethnomusicologicum 4. 221–44.

Vickers, Adrian. 1985. "The Realm of the Senses: Images of the Court Music of Pre-Colonial Bali." *Imago Musicae* 2:143–77.

Vitale, Wayne. 2002. "Balinese *Kebyar* Music Breaks the Five-Tone Barrier: New Composition for Seven-Tone *Gamelan*", *Perspectives of New Music* 40(1): 5–69.

Vitale, Wayne. 1990. "Kotekan: the Technique of Interlocking Parts in Balinese Music", *Balungan,* iv/2: 2–16.

Recordings of Balinese Music

Since the 1920s, when recordings of gamelan sparked Colin McPhee into going to Bali, there has been a steady stream of international releases. Arbiter Records has reissued some of those McPhee heard, with excellent notes by Ed Herbst *(The Roots of Gamelan;* www.arbiterrecords.com). More recent issues feature improved recording quality, are careful to include complete compositions and ensembles, and provide well-researched notes. Yet many of the good ones listed in the previous edition of this book are now hard to find or no longer available, so ironically there is less to choose from now than there was in the 1990s. In the following I provide some suggestions for recordings of gamelan beyond those included on the enclosed CD.

Recordings made and sold in Bali. In the 1970s-'90s cassette companies flourished in Bali and they were practically comprehensive in their coverage. The combined catalogs of *Bali Stereo, Aneka, Maharani* and other companies listed thousands of releases of village and Festival gamelan. Many but not all now appear on CD. In shops like Ubud Music (on the main road in Ubud), tucked in among all the DVDs and international pop music, compilations packaged for tourists with titles like *The Legong Dance* or *The Best of Barong* may satisfy those looking just for a taste of gamelan. But my hope is that if you have this book you'll wish to go deeper. In that case look for CDs devoted to particular groups such as the ones mentioned in the book: the gamelan gong kebyar of Perean, Pindha, or Gladag villages, the semar pegulingan of Binoh, gender wayang of Sukawati, selunding of Tenganan. Most of the Festival Gong competitors are represented on CD as well.

Internationally distributed recordings. As mentioned, stock and availabilities change often. Below are listed some of the better ones available as of late 2010 at a selection of online sources. iTunes and amazon.com can also be consulted for some of the same music.

- At www.cdbaby.com: *Odalan Bali* by gamelan Çudamani made on their 2007 North America tour, *Bali South: Gamelan Gong Kebyar and Gamelan Angklung*, a compilation of music recorded in the 1960s published by the UCLA Ethnomusicology archive; *I Madé Subandi: Wayang Babad,* a suite of new compositions by contemporary composer Subandi; *Gamelan of Munduk Village,* a recording from the northern

Bali kebyar stronghold of Munduk. The site also features releases by international gamelan ensembles such as Gita Asmara, Giri Kedaton and Gadung Kasturi.

- The Nonesuch Explorer Series (www.nonesuch.com) introduced many to the sounds of world music in the 1970s and they continue to make their classic recordings available. Among them: *Bali: Music from the Morning of the World; Bali: Gamelan and Kecak; Bali: Golden Rain;* and *Bali: Gamelan Semar Pegulingan.* The last features the musicians from Teges mentioned in Chapter Six.

- Classics Online (www.classicsonline.com) features recommended CDs on the Celestial Harmonies label (Music of Bali vols. 1–3, with gamelan jegog, gong kebyar, and others), a rare recording of gamelan semar pegulingan from East Bali on the Wergo label, and the incomparably sweet semar pegulingan of Ketewel village on Lyrichord.

- At www.discogs.com recordings from the Ocora label can be found, among them *Bali: Gamelan Joged Bumbung, Bali: Gong Gdé of Batur, Bali: Sebatu—les Danses Masquées* (music for masked dances played on gong kebyar) and *Les Grands Gong Kebyars des Années Soixante,* an excellent kebyar compilation from the 1960s including a few tracks of the Pindha group at their storied peak.

- Vital Records (www.vitalrecords.ws) a small label devoted solely to Balinese gamelan and founded by specialist Wayne Vitale, offers some choice recordings. *Çudamani* features the incomparable sanggar playing Dewa Ketut Alit's *Geregel.* There are excellent releases of gamelan gambuh and gong kebyar as well.

- Finally, at folkways.si.edu (Smithsonian Folkways) there is little from Bali but the extraordinary 20-CD compilation *Music of Indonesia*, compiled by master scholar Philip Yampolsky between 1990 and 2000, offers an unequalled audio tour of music throughout the archipelago, much of which had never been recorded before.

Videos and DVDs of Balinese music are easily had in Bali, and there are many good performances to see on You Tube and other online hubs. As with audio, seek out DVDs focused on a specific group or style rather than slapped-together compilations. Online videos multiply quickly; obviously discernment is required. Of special note is historical footage (search You Tube for Bali 1910, 1932, 1946 and others), some of which has music recorded *in situ* at the time.

Glossary

angklung (ahng-*kloong*); a bamboo rattle, now uncommon in Bali, that produces a single pitch when shaken.

angsel (ahng-*sul*); a sharp, sudden dance movement or musical accent.

angsel bawak (ahng-*sul* bah-*wahk*); a short *angsel* that is prepared, executed and completed within two gong cycles.

angsel lantang (ahng-*sul* lahn-*tahng*); a long angsel, prepared, executed and completed over several cycles; usually it is the climax of the performance.

arja (ahr-*jha*); a Balinese theatrical form combining dance, singing, indigenous stories, and comedy.

ASTI See ISI

balai banjar (bah *lay* bahn-*jahr*); the village ward meeting hall, ordinarily the storage and rehearsal space for the gamelan.

Bali Arts Festival A yearly event, held at the Denpasar Art Center in June and July, that was initiated by Balinese Governor Ida Bagus Mantra in 1979 as a showcase for new and traditional performing, literary, culinary and plastic arts.

banjar (bahn-*jahr*); village ward; community organization.

bapang (bah-*pahng*); a colotomic cycle of 4 or 8 beats punctuated in the middle by the *klentong*.

Baris (bah-*riss*); a genre of male warrior dances; also specifically refers to the solo Baris dance popular today.

Baris Cina (bah-*riss* chee-*nha*); a sacred Baris performed only at certain ceremonies in Renon village.

Baris gdé (bah-*riss* g'*day*); one of several group Baris choreographies with sacred functions.

Barong (bah-*rong*); the Balinese protector-dragon.

batel (bah-*tell*); battle music; also one of several possible colotomic structures used to underpin such music.

bebende (b'-ben-*day*); a medium sized gong with a flattened boss sometimes used for colotomic punctuation.

byong (bee-*yong*); an explosive *kebyar* attack which includes the sound of eight *reyong* pots played together.

cak (cha'); a performance genre portraying a climactic episode from the Ramayana epic. A chorus of men surrounding dancers imitate the sounds of a monkey army with percussive noises and interlocking vocal rhythms.

cakepung (cha-k'-*poong*); a choral imitation of the sounds of the *gamelan*, performed informally in northern and eastern Bali.

Calonarang (cha-lohn-ah-*rhang*); a Balinese tale of sorcery and possession performed as a drama, usually with *gamelan pelegongan* accompaniment.

calung (cha-*loong*); the middle-register instrument that plays the core melody tones.

cengceng (cheng-*cheng*); a set of small cymbals used in most gamelan.

cengceng kopyak (cheng-*cheng* ko-*pya'*); large crash cymbals used in ceremonial music.

colotomy; colotomic structure the technique of using gongs to mark important structural points in music; the arrangement of gong strokes in a given melody.

condong (chohn-*dong*); attendant to a princess or queen, a character found in many performance genres, notably the *legong keraton* dances.

dag (dhag); the deep sound made with either a *panggul* (mallet) or the palm of the right hand on the kendang wadon.

dalang (dah-*lhang*); storyteller or puppeteer.

ding, dong, deng, dung, dang solfege names of the tones in Balinese tuning systems.

dolanan (do-*lahn*-an); children's songs and song-games.

drama gong a theatrical form portraying contemporary stories, popular since the 1960s.

dug (doog); the deep sound (but not so deep as *dag*) made with a panggul (mallet) playing on the right head of the *kendang lanang*.

Festival Gong the yearly Bali-wide *gamelan gong kebyar* competition.

gabor (gah-*bohr*); a genre of female offering dances. Also called Pendet in some areas.

gamelan (gah-*mel*-an); set of instruments; orchestra.

gamelan angklung a delicate four-tone ensemble used mainly in temple ceremonies and processions.

gamelan bebonangan (b'-bo-*nang*-an); a marching gamelan with gongs, drums and cymbals.

gamelan baleganjur (b'-le-*ghan*-joor); see gamelan bebonangan.

gamelan gambang (gam-*bahng*); an ancient and sacred seven-tone ensemble using font wooden-keyed instruments and two metal *saron*. (See also saron.)

gamelan gambuh (gam-*booh*); one of the oldest extant gamelan types. The ensemble is comprised of large flutes, *rebab*, and percussion; it accompanies theatrical settings of old Javanese stories.

gamelan gandrung (gan-*droong*); a once-popular bamboo ensemble used to accompany street dances.

gamelan gender wayang (g'n-*dare* wah-*yang*); four-piece, *slendro*-tuned ensemble used mainly to accompany the shadow play.

gamelan gong bheri (bh'*ree*); a gamelan of gongs and drums found only in the village of Renon and used to accompany the Baris Cina dance.

gamelan gong a scaled-down version of the *gamelan gong gdé* that was common during the decades prior to the emergence of kebyar.

gamelan gong gdé (g'-*day*); the largest Balinese gamelan, important in the courts during the feudal era.

gamelan gong kebyar (k'-*byahr*); the standard modern concert gamelan, important for both sacred and secular functions.

gamelan jegog (j'-*gog*); a 4-tone gamelan made from gigantic stalks of bamboo, found solely in the western district of Jembrana.

gamelan joged bumbung (jo-*ged* boom-*boong*); a slendro-tuned bamboo ensemble that plays instrumental music and accompanies the *joged* dance.

gamelan luang (lwang); a rare and sacred seven-tone ensemble.

gamelan pelegongan (p'le-*gong*-an); a five-tone derivative of the *gamelan semar pegulingan* used mainly in accompanying the legong keraton dances.

gamelan selonding (s'lohn-*ding*); a sacred gamelan of iron keys, found in many eastern Bali Aga villages.

gamelan semar pegulingan (s'*mar* p'-goo-*ling*-ahn); a bronze seven-tone ensemble of the royal courts; also a five-tone version of the same.

gangsa (gahng-sah); a middle-register metallophone used to play melodic ornamentation.

gegaboran (g'gah-*bohr*-an); a colotomic structure used in *gabor* dance forms and *tari lepas* (see gabor).

gender (g'n-*dare*); any metallophone constructed so that the keys are suspended over bamboo resonators; more specifically the term is used to connote *gender* that are played with two mallets, one in each hand.

gending (g'n-*ding*); musical composition.

genggong (g'n-*gong*); a kind of jaw harp.

gilak (ghee-*lahk*); a colotomic pattern important in male dances and processional music.

gineman (ghee-*num*-an); a rhapsodic, free introduction to an instrumental composition.

gotong royong (go-tong row-*yohng*); mutual help, community service.

grantang (gran-*tahng*); see tingklik.

ISI (formerly STSI, and before that ASTI); the government college/conservatory of the performing arts in Denpasar.

jauk (jowk); a masked dance portraying a demonic character.

jegogan (j'*go*-gahn); the deepest-toned keyed instruments; used to stress important notes in the cote melody.

jublag (joo-*blag*); alternate name for the *calung*.

kabupaten (kha-boo-pah-*ten*); government region or district. Bali has eight; they are Badung, Bangli, Buleleng, Gianyar, Jembrana, Karangasem, Klungkung, and Tabanan.

kajar (kha-*jahr*); (from the verb *ajar*, to teach) a colotomic instrument that mimics drum rhythms in some styles of music.

kakawin (k'kah-*win*); vocal music sung from texts in palm-leaf manuscripts and written in Kawi, the old Javanese language.

kantilan (kahn-*teel*-an); the highest-pitched instruments in the *gangsa* section.

kap the slapping sound made with the left hand on the *kendang wadon*

karawitan (k'rah-wee-*tahn*); a general term for the art of gamelan and gamelan music.

kebyar (k'-*byahr*); abbreviation for gamelan gong kebyar or its music; also a violent, rhythmically irregular passage played by a full gamelan in unison.

Kebyar Duduk (dhoo-*dhook*); A tari lepas choreographed by Maria in the 1920s that is performed in a sitting position.

Kebyar Trompong (trohm-|*pong*); A tari lepas choreographed hy Maria in which the dancer performs on the *trompong*.

kecak (khe-cha'); see cak.

kelenang (k'le-*nahng*); tiny colotomic instrument that falls between heats in some older styles of music.

kempli (k'*m-plee*); horizontal gong, hand held or mounted on a stand, that is primarily used to keep a steady beat.

kempur (k'm-*poor*); medium sized hanging gong that is used to demarcate important structural points in melodies.

kendang (k 'n-*dahng*); the cylindrical, two-headed Balinese drum, held across the lap and played with both hands.

kendang mabarung (k 'n-*dahng* m'*bah*-roong); an ensemble featuring gigantic drums that is popular in west Bali.

kerawang (k'rah-*wang*); the bronze alloy used in casting gongs and keys.

ketua sekaha gong (k'twa s'kha gong); administrative head of a gamelan club.

kidung (khee-*dhoong*); a type of sacred vocal music based mostly on old Balinese poetry; also the singing style associated with kidung.

klentong (kl'n *tohng*); small hanging gong often used to mark the midpoints of melodies.

KOKAR/SMKI the Balinese high school of the performing arts, located in Batubulan.

kotekan (kho-*te*'-ahn); melodic ornamentation composed of two interlocking musical parts. (See also *polos*, *sangsih*)

kreasi baru (k'ray-ah-si bah-*rhoo*); new compositions or choreographies.

lagu (lah-*ghoo*); melody.

lanang (lah-*nhang*); male. Refers to the higher-pitched of a pair of gongs or drums. eg., kendang lanang, *gong lanang*. (See also *wadon*)

Lasem (lah-*s'm*); a Javanese legend enacted in one of the *legong* choreographies; also the name of a *lelambatan* composition in *tabuh kutus* form.

latihan (lah-*tee*-han); a rehearsal. (Indonesian)

legong bidedari (l'*gong* bee-d'*dah*-ree); a progenitor of the legong ketaton performed in Ketewel village.

legong keraton (l'*gong* k'rah-*tohn*); a group of classical dance suites performed by pairs of young girls or women, often performed with a prelude danced by the condong.

lelambatan (l'lahm-*bha*-tahn); a family of classical instrumental compositions performed primarily in the temple to entertain visiting deities.

LISTIBIYA (lis-*tih*-b'ya); the Balinese Government Council on the Arts.

lontar (lohn-*tahr*); palm leaf manuscripts.

mabarung (m'*bah*-roong); to play together in competition style.

muruk (moo-roo'); a rehearsal. (Balinese)

nangka or ketewel (nahng-kha); an indigenous semi-hard wood used to carve drums and instrument frames.

nuutin (n 'woo-*tin*); (from the verb *tuut*, to follow) a simple *kotekan* pattern in which the sangsih alternates with the polos on the next highest tone.

odalan (o-*dahl*-ahn); Balinese temple anniversary ceremonies. They occur once in each 210 day calendrical cycle and are marked by three days of festivities that often include music and dance performances.

Oleg Tambulilingan (o-leg tahm-boo-*lil*-ing-ahn); a choreography of Maria's from the early 1950s depicting the courtship of two bumblebees in a garden of flowers.

oncang-oncangan (ohn-*chahng* ohn-*chahng*-ahn); percussive interjections in kebyar music created by the composite sounds of drums, *cengceng*, and eight of the reyong pots played together to form a chord.

pak (pah'); the slapping sound made with the left hand on the kendang lanang.

panggul (pahng-*gool*); mallet.

pelawah (p'lah-*wah*); wooden musical instrument frame.

pélog (peh *lohg*); a seven tone tuning system, with many five-tone derivatives, that is used throughout Bali and Java.

pemadé (p'mah-*day*); the middle-range instruments of the gangsa section.

pemungkah (p'moong-*kah*); opening music for the shadow play, performed while the *dalang* introduces the puppets to the world of the screen.

penabuh (p'nah-*booh*); gamelan musician (see also *tabuh*)

pengawak (p'ng-ah-*wa*'); (from *awak*, body) main movement of a musical composition.

penyacah (p'nyah-*chah*); an instrument used in some gamelan that is one octave higher than the calung and plays at twice their rate.

polos (po-*lohss*); the component of kotekan that is closely related to the core melody tones. (See also sangsih, kotekan)

preret (p'ray-*ret*); a reedy trumpet found in east Bali and Lombok.

Rangda (rhang-*dha*); witch-mother; nemesis of the Barong.

rebab (r'*bahb*); a two-string bowed instrument.

rejang (r'*jahng*); a sacred ceremonial dance for women.

reyong (r'*yhong*); instrument consisting of a row of tuned small gongs arranged in scalar order on a long frame that is played by pairs of musicians. The reyong in the gamelan gong kebyar is played by four people.

rindik (rin-*dhi'*); see *tingklik*.

sangsih (sahng-*sih*); the component of kotekan that is created by interlocking with the polos. (See also kotekan, polos)

saron (sah-*rhon*); any metallophone constructed so that the keys are held in place by posts and laid over a trough. (Also called *gangsa jongkok*.)

sekaha (s'*kha*); club or organization.

seledet (s'le-*deht*); dance movement consisting of a rapid side-to-side flick of the eyes.

selisir (s'lee-*sihr*); one of the five-tone modes derived from the *pélog* tuning system.

sendratari (s'n-dra-*tah*-ree); dance-drama; a modern amalgam of traditional stories and a variety of music and dance types.

sisya (see-sya); in the Calonarang story, the apprentices of the sorceress.

slanketan (s'lahn-k'-*tahn*); an ornamentation style of the *gamelan jegog*.

slendro (s'len-*dhro*); a tuning system found throughout Java and Bali that is theoretically based on the division of the octave into five equal parts.

suling (soo-ling); bamboo flute.

sunaren (soo-nah-*rhen*); one of the five-tone modes derived from the pélog tuning system.

tabuh (ta-*booh*); composition, musical form, also used as a verb (*menabuh*) meaning 'to play', (see also *penabuh*)

taksu (tahk-*soo*); performance charisma. Balinese believe in an individual's innate, inherited ability to make an audience enjoy a performance.

tari lepas (tah-ree l'*pahss*); (lit. free dances) brief modern dances unconnected to larger theatrical forms.

Taruna Jaya (t'roo-nah jah-*yha*); a tari lepas depicting the capricious moods of a youth on the verge of adulthood.

tawa-tawa a small gong used in the *gamelan angklung*.

tektekan (te'-*te'*-ahn); ensemble similar to *gamelan baleganjur* using bamboo sticks instead of or in addition to gongs and cengceng.

tembang (t'*m-bahng)*; a family of verse forms.

tembung (t'm-buhng); one of the five-tone modes derived from the pélog tuning system.

tingklik (ting-*kli'*); an instrument of bamboo tubes suspended in a wooden frame; also known as *grantang* or *rindik*.

topeng (to-*peng*); masked dance.

trompong (trohm-*pong*); instrument consisting of a row of tuned small gongs arranged in scalar order on a long frame that is played by a single musician.

tukang (too-*khang)*; someone that performs an activity. *Tukang kendang*: drummer; tukang reyong; reyong player; etc.

tut (toot); the deep sound (but not so deep as dag) made with the palm of the right hand on the kendang lanang.

ugal (oo-*ghal)*; the lead gangsa.

wadon (wah-*dohn*); female. Refers to the lower-pitched of a pair of gongs or drums, eg., kendang wadon, gong wadon. (See also lanang)

wayang kulit (wah-yhang koo-*lit*); the shadow puppet play.

Index

Page numbers in italics denotes photo/drawing

A

A Club of Small Men 121
A House in Bali 154
Agama Hindu Dharma 15, 146
Alit, I Dewa Ketut 126, 132–5, *133*, 149, 154
angklung 13, 97–8, 171
angklung kebyar 98
Angklungan, a composition 65
angsel 60, 64, 71, *80*, 81, 83, 88, 106–7, 118, 128, 171
angsel bawak diagram 82
angsel bawak 82, 83, 171
angsel lantang 82, 83, 171
Arakok, a composition 154
Ardha Chandra open theater 140
arja 111, 119, 133, 171
Arini Alit, Ni Ketut 10
Asak village 103, 105
Asnawa, Ketut tide, composer 10, 106
AST1 (now ISI) 30, 171, 174
Astita, Komang 10, 66

B

balai banjar 116, 120, 137, 139, 141, 171
balai taksu 121, 160
baleganjur 106–8
Bali Aga, composition for *gamelan selonding* 104
Bali Aga gamelan 103–4
Bali Arts Festival 31, 124, 140, 143, 148, 171
Balinese music abroad 142–4
Balinese musical instruments 39–46
Balinese musical organizations 115–7
bamboo gamelan ensembles 99–103
bamboo instrument(s) 45–6, 85, 99, 105
bamboo resonator(s) 35, 39, 102, 174

Bandem, Dr. Madé, head of ISI (formerly STSI), 10, 126, 129–132, *130*, 137
Bangli district 98–9, 128, 174
Banjar Abiankapas, Denpasar 93
Banjar Kalah, Peliatan village 100, 117
Banjar Tampak Gangsul, Denpasar 92
banjar 16, 20, 93, 107, 116–7, 119, 123, 133, 139, 142, 148–9, 152–3, 159, 171
bapang 62, 83, 171
Baris dance music 67–83
Baris 9, 68–9, 71, 74–5, 78–9, 81, 83, 89, 137, 171
Baris Cina (Chinese Baris) 105, 171, 173
Baris gdé 171
Baris kotekan 75
Barong 56, 93, 137, 171, 177
batel 62, 171
batu malablab (idiom for poor playing) 17
Batuan village, Gianyar 24, 151, 155
Batubulan village 139, 151, 175
Batubulan village performances 137
bawak and lantang *angsels* 81–3
bebende 43, 171
bebonangan 62, 106
Begeg, I Wayan of Pangkung, Tabanan 92
Belaluan village near Denpasar 90, 92
Beratha, I Wayan, drummer and composer 10, 92, 155, 157
"bimusicality" 142
bhoma (earth spirits) 35
Binoh village 94
Blahbatuh village, Gianyar 27, 33, 90, 126, 128
Blangsinga village, Gianyar 92, 126
Bona village 108
bonang 106

Borobudur bas-reliefs 23
bronze gamelan ensembles 87–99
Bugbug village *xvi* (color inserts)
byong 71, 171

C

cak (monkey chant) 107–8
cakepung 109, 172
Calonarang play 93, 172, 177
calung 39, *41,* 48, 49, 51–2, 55, 59,
    70–1, 74, 76, 89, 92, 98, 101, 172,
    174, 176
Canderi, I Madé 10
Capung Manjus (Bathing Dragonfly),
    a composition 97
Caru Wara, a composition 132
Catra, I Nyoman 10
cengceng 40, 44, 49, 60, 62, 81–2,
    88, 97–8, 103, 105–6, 108–9, 172,
    176–7
cengceng kopyak 40, 44, 62, 106–7,
    172
ceremonial music 15, 44, 60–4,
    172
Cerucuk Punyah (Drunken Cerucuk
    Bird), a composition 97
Children and Music in Bali 121,
    167
children and music 13, 120–2
classical poetry verse forms as base for
    musical structure 65, 105
Coast, John, British entrepreneur 20,
    162
colonial period 27–29, 93, 102
coloromic notation for *gilak* 73
colotomic structure(s) 49, 50, 62, 64,
    172–4
commissioning performances 139
communication between dancer and
    gamelan 56, 81
competition(s) 90, 101 107, 112,
    122–3, 143, 148, 176
composition(s) 60–7, 85, 89–90,
    93–7, 101, 103–5, 112, 132, 137,
    149–50, 154, 168, 174–7

condong 64, 172, 175
conservatories 86, 91, 93, 104, 124,
    129, 139–40, 142
conservatory group(s) 91
Cooper, Rachel 10
coordination in gamelan 17, 58,
    69–70, 114-5
core melody 25, 42, 48–9, 51–5,
    58–60, 65, 71, 74–6, 82–3, 105, 117,
    172, 177
court music 98
Covarrubias, Miguel 87
cremation(s) 95, 104
cue(s) for changes 56, *57,* 58–60, 63,
    71, 82–3, 128
cultural exchange 131
cyclical regenerative musical time
    48–9
cyclical structure 65
cymbals 24, 39, 44, 92, 109, 172

D

dalang 95–6, 172, 176
Debussy, Claude 19
Demong, I Madé 10
Demulih village near Bangli 99
Denpasar 9, 24, 26, 29–31, 33, 66, 84,
    90–94, 96, 99, 102, 105–106, 121,
    124, 128–129, 139, 148, 153, 155,
    157–158
Denpasar Art Center 140, 171
Depehe village, east of Singaraja 24
Dewa Nyoman Batuan 10
Dewa Nyoman Sura, drummer *ii–iii*
    (color inserts)
Dibia, I Wayan, choreographer 10,
    108
dissemination of court music to
    villages 98
diversity of gamelan types 84
dolanan (children's songs) 122, 172
drama gong(s) 119, 172
drummer(s) 10, 56, 58, 71, 81–2,
    89–90, 102, 106, 115, 121, 126, 128,
    133, 158

drum(s) 14, 16, 18, 24–5, 33, 39, 44, 46, 56, 58, 60, 62, 71, 76, 79, 81–2, 89, 95–8, 100, 105, 107, 109, 111, 117, 121–2, 126, 128, 156–7, 173–7

E
Eka Dasa Rudra 55
ensemble coordination 23, 58
Es (Ice), a composition 132

F
female *gong kebyar sekaha* 122
Festival Gong gamelan competitions 91, 112, 122, 124, 128, 133, 139, 148, 154, 172
flute(s) (see also *suling)* 14, 16, 24, 39, 45–46, 72, 100
folk music 99
foreign students 131, 136, 141, 149
form 60-4

G
Gableran, Pandé Made *26,* 10, 33–5
gabor offering dance 50, 172–3
Gama Astawa, I Wayan 10
Gambang Suling, a composition 90
Gambangan*,* a composition 65
gambang compositions 105
"*gambangan* rhythm" 105
gambelan 16
gambuh 24–26, 36–37, 124, 155
   ensemble 25
   gambuh composition(s) 24–5
gamelan 8–9, 13–17, 19–31, 33, 35–9, 42–5, 49, 51–2, 54, 56, 59–60, 62, 65–6, 68, 70–1, 81–6, 87, 89–95, 97–8, 102–6, 109, 112, 114–20, 123–4, 126, 129, 131–2, 134, 136–7, 139, 142, 144, 148–9, 151–2, 154–6, 158–9, 172–7
   Balinese gamelan 10, 21, 24–5, 36, 39, 48, 58, 67, 96, 99, 109, 119, 126, 142–3, 149, 156, 173
   definition 16
   gamelan club(s) 29, 175

gamelan competitions (see also Festival Gong) 15, 31, 122
gamelan composition(s) 16, 48
gamelan ensemble(s) 17, 87–103, 143, 149
gamelan festivals 150
gamelan foundry(ies) 33–4
gamelan gambuh 24–25, 46, 64, 92, 103–4, 151, 173
gamelan group(s) 16, 114, 119, 139, 143, 150, 156
gamelan instruments 16, 33, 36, 120, 136, 142,
gamelan maker 33
gamelan miscellany 108
gamelan museum 151
gamelan music 7, 9, 16–19, 31, 38, 43, 49, 65, 109, 111, 118, 136–7, 147–8, 156, 175
gamelan musician(s) 31, 55, 176
gamelan organization(s) 10, 116
gamelan performance(s) 15, 17, 44, 58, 138
gamelan players 118, 152
gamelan tour(s) 128
gamelan tuner 155
gamelan workshop 158
Javanese gamelan 9, 104, 142
gamelan angklung *14,* 37, 42, 64–5, 96–8, 121, 139, 143, 159, 172, 178
gamelan baleganjur 62, 106–7, 173, 178
gamelan batel 109
gamelan bebonangan 173
gamelan gambang 65, 104–5, 151, 173
   playing at a cremation *ix* (color inserts)
gamelan gandrung 102, 173
gamelan geguntangan 111
gamelan gender wayang 37, 65, 84, 94–6, 100, 158–9, 173
gamelan gender wayang batel *113*
Gamelan Gita Asmara 8
gamelan gong 98–9, 173

gamelan gong bheri 105–6, 173
gamelan gong gdé (great gong) 26, 44, 62, 98–9, 105–6, 124, 151–2, 173
gamelan gong kebyar (see also *kebyar*) i (color inserts), 28–9, 35, 66, 68, 84, 87, 87–92, 97, 99, 108, 112, 143, 148, 158, 173, 173–4
gamelan in Java 22
Gamelan Jagat Anyar 8
gamelan jegog 109, 173, 177
gamelan jogged 65, 100–2
gamelan joged bumbung 65, 99–101, 140, 173
gamelan luang 105–6, 173
gamelan pelegongan 28, 64, 92–4, 105, 173
gamelan sekaha 116
Gamelan Sekar Jaya 8, 11, 156
Gamelan Sekar Kembar 11
gamelan selonding 103, 173
gamelan selunding xvi (color inserts), 111
gamelan semar pegulingan 26, 37, 64, 92, 173
gamelan semaradana 154–6
Gandera, I Wayan 11
gangsa 39, 49, 59, 60, 70, 82, 83, 89, 98, 115, 117, 141, 173–4, 176
gangsa kotekan 115
gangsa jongkok 39, 177
Gantas, I Ketut 11
gegaboran 50–1, 62, 173
geguritan 111
Geladag village group 90–1, 128
gender family 39–43
gender 174
gender wayang 42, 95–6, 100, 102, 109, 140, 158–9
gender wayang compositions 96
gending 16, 174
gending sanghyang 112
genggong 46, 109, 174
Geregel, a composition 132
Gianyar district 24, 33, 90, 92, 98, 100, 102, 105, 108, 174

gilak 60, 62, 71, 73, 83, 106, 118, 174
gineman 89, 174
Goak Maling Taloh (Crow Steals Eggs), a composition 97
giying (or *ugal*) 39
gong ageng 43
gong kebyar 36, 43, 87, 98, 106, 133, 140, 155
gong kebyar groups 133
gong pattern(s) 51, 60, 73
gong suling ensemble 109
gongan 49, 51, 60, 68, 71
gongan structure(s) 50, 52, 81
gong(s) 2, 14, 16–7, 22, 24–6, 29, 33–4, 39, 43–4, 46, 48–53, 58, 60, 62–4, 69–71, 73–6, 82–3, 85, 88, 92, 95–8, 100, 105–6, 109, 111, 114, 117, 152–3, 155, 158, 172–6, 177–8
bossless gongs 106
gotong royong 116, 174
grantang (see *tingklik*)
Grindem, 1 Madé 11, 94
Griya, Anak Ayung Putu 11
Griya, I Madé 11, 157
guntang 46, 111

H

Hendrawan, Cokorda Alit 11
Hindu mythology 23, 155
Hindu-Balinese religion 15
Hood, Mantle, ethnomusicologist 11, 142

I

improvisation 23, 54, 59, 111
incep 17
individuality 86
Indonesian independence 29, 99
instrument case carvers 34
interaction of music with dance 80–3
interlocking parts (see also *kotekan*) 54, 75
iron gamelan 103–4
ISI (formerly STSI) 30, 86, 128–31, 134, 139, 142, 152–3, 171, 174

J

Jagaraga village28, 90
Jauk dance 56, 62, 174
Javanese court music 23
Jaya Semara, a composition 90
Jebeg, I Wayan 11
Jimat, I Madé 11
jegogan 39, *40*, 48–9, 51–2, 55, 62,
    70–1, 74, 89, 92, 97, 98, 101, 115,
    123, 174
Jembrana district 101–2, 173–4
joged dance 100, 173
jublag 39, 174

K

kabupaten 26, 28, 91, 174,
kajar 43, 49, 64, 92, 174
kakawin 22, 26, 110–2, 151, 155, 158,
    175
Kaler, Nyoman, composer/choreogra-
    pher 102
Kaliungu Kaja, Denpasar 106, 153
Kamasan village, Klungkung 92
kantilan *41*, 42, 70, 73–4, 88, 155,
    174
Kapi Raja, a composition 90
karawitan 16, 174
Katak Nongkek (Croaking Frog), a
    composition 97
Kawi, old Javanese language 110–1,
    174
kebyar 28–9, 31, 65, 86–94, 99,
    101–2, 105, 129, 131, 137, 151, 154,
    155–9, 171, 173–4, 176
kebyar drummer(s) 58, 156
Kebyar Duduk *27*, 88, 174
Kebyar Gandrung *12*
Kebyar Legong 89
Kebyar Trompong 88, 174
kebyar groups, number of 131
kecak 107–8, 175
Kedewatan village *14*
kelenang 43, 175
kemong (see *klentong*)
kempli 43, 49, 50, *51*, 52, 54–6,
    59–60, 62–4, 69 71, 73–6, 79, 81–3,
    89, 92, 97, 106–7, 117, 175
kempur *32, 41*, 43, 49–50, 60, 62–4,
    73–4, 76, 82, 92, 97, 175
kendang *44, 51*, 44–5, 49, 56, 58–60,
    62, 64, 69, 71, 76, 79, 81–3, 88, 92,
    106, 128, 141, 175
kendang lanang 172, 175–6, 178
kendang mabarung 109, 175
kendang patterns 78–81
kendang wadon 172, 174, 178
Kerambitan, Tabanan 94, 98, 105
kerawang 34, 175
Keredek, I Madé 129
Ketapian Kelod, Denpasar 102
Ketewel village 94, 170, 175
ketewel (or nangka wood) 34, 44, 176
ketua sekaha gong 139, 175
kidung 26, 64, 110–2, 175
klentong *32, 41*, 43, 49, 50, 64, 171,
    175
Klungkung 92, 105, 174
KOKAR/SMKI 29, 86, 94, 96, 139,
    142, 175
KOKAR High School of Music and
    Dance 9, 30, 128
Konderi, Ni Wayan 11
Konolan, I Wayan 11, 96, 157–8
Kosalia Arini, a composition 90
kotekan 52, 54–6, 59–60, 64–6, 69,
    75, 78, 83, 86, 89, 91, 95, 97–8,
    100–2, 104, 106–7, 115–6, 118,
    140–1, 175–7
kreasi baleganjur 107
kreasi baru 66, 89–90, 98, 123, 175
Kumpul, I Ketut 11

L

lagu 16, 175
Lake Batur temple 99
Laksmi, Desak Madé 11, 122, 154
lanang (male *kendang*) 44, 56, 71, 76,
    175, 178
Lasem story 93, 159, 175
Lastini, Ni Putu 11

latihan 175
learning Balinese music 117–9, 140-4
Lebah, I Madé of Peliatan 11, 94, 133
legong bidedari 94, 175
legong dance(s) 28, 27
legong dancers 94
legong keraton 93, 172, 175
lelambatan 26, 53, 62–4, 87, 91, 96,
    98, 105, 123, 139, 158–9, 175
lelambatan pengawak 62
LISTIB1YA 137, 176
Loceng, I Wayan "gender king" 11,
    96, *xiii* (color inserts)
lontar 23–4, 26, 109, 176
Lotring, I Wayan (composer/teacher)
    28, 65, 93–4
Lumbung, I Gusti 11

M
mabarung 101, 109, 176
Madra, Ketut (painter) 7, 9, 11
Mahabharata epic 35, 95
Malat, epic poem 24
Mandera, Anak Agung Gdé 11, 157
Manik, Gdé 11, 28, 90, 157
marching bands 106
Maria, I Ketut, dancer *27*, 88
Mas, Cokorda 11
Mas village 97, 113
matetekep 17
McPhee, Colin 14, *15,* 19–21, 28, 93,
    94, 121, 142, 154, 157
Mead, Margaret, anthropologist 20
melodic content 49
melodic cycles 25, 101
melodic ideas 62
melodic instruments 111
melodic line 49
melodic loops 53
melodic ornamentation (see also *kote-
    kan*) 19, 173, 175
melodic ornaments 62
melodic parts 69, 72–4, 116
melodic passages 17
melodic phrases 62

melodic range 111
melodic role 43
melodic snippets 89
melodic style 43, 98, 105, 109
melodic techniques 154
melodic variation 58
melody framework 49
memorization 119
Merak Ngelo, a composition 95, 160
metallophones 16, 24, 39, 42–3, 46,
    88, 97, 105–6, 173–4, 177
metalsmith *(pandé)* 33
Monkey Chant 107
Munduk 92, 96
muruk 176
music and dance 8, 15, 20, 29, 66, 81,
    88, 130–2, 137, 143, 148, 176–7
Music in Bali 21
music in Balinese society 114–24
music schools 139, 142
musical form(s) 60–6, 89, 172
musicians 8, 10–11, 17, 19–20, 22–3,
    28–31, 33, 36, 43, 47–50, *52*, 53, 55,
    58–9, 63, 66–9, 75, 82, 85–6, 88–9,
    91–2, 95–6, 100–2, 105, 108, 111,
    114–9, 121, 123, 125–6, 128–32,
    134–42, 144, 150–5, 157–9, 177–8
musik kontemporer 66, 152, 154

N
Naga (mythical serpents) 35
Nartha, *dalang xiii* (color inserts)
Navadaza, a composition 154
Negara, Ida Bagus Raka 11
*norot (*or *nuutin)* 54, 176

O
odalan 139, 176
offerings before performance *138*
older gamelan 64–6
Oleg Tambulilingan *i* (color inserts)
    89, 176
oncang-oncangan 122, 176
oral tradition 23
ornamental figuration (see *kotekan*)

ostinato(s) (short, repeating melodies) 64, 102
  Baris ostinato 71
  gilak ostinato 118

P

Padangkertha, Karangasem 96
Pager, Pandé Wayan 33
pandé clan 33
panggul (mallets) 39, 44, 172, 176
Panji, I Gusti Ngurah 11
Panji, prince 24, 110
Pareg 126
payment for lessons 141
Pedungan, near Denpasar 24
pelawah (instrument cases) 34–5, 176
Peliatan village 7–9, 20–1, 30, 89–90, 94, 96, 100, 112, 117, 122, 133, 159
pélog 36–8, 65, 68–9, 88, 92–3, 96, 98, 101–3, 156, 176–7
pemadé 39, *40*, *41*, 42, *70*, 70, 73–4, 88, 155, 176
Pemungkah, a composition 95, 176
penabuh 176–7
pengawak 62–4, 159, 176
penyacah 39, 176
Perean village, Tahanan 91, 150
Pindha village (sekaha) 10, 128
Pogog, I Wayan 11, 157
polos 54–6, 75–6, 78, 175–7
polos and *sangsih* 54–6, 75, 91, 101, 106
pondok 7
preret (reedy trumpet) 46, 177
processional gamelan (see also marching) 62
pupuh 111–2
puppeteer(s) (see also *dalang*) 65, 95–6, 110, 158, 172

R

Rai, I Wayan 11
Rajeg of Tunjuk, Tabanan 96
Raka, Anak Agung Gde of Saba village 11, 94

Ramayana epic 35, 107, 109, 154, 172
Rangda 93, 137, 177
Rara Kadiri, poetic meters 111
rebab 24–5, 39, *41*, 46, 49, 54, 62, 126, 152, 173, 177
regional variation 69, 85, 96
Regog, Madé 11, 92, 157
rehearse/rehearsal(s) 10, 16, 49, 56, 59, 90, 102, 114–8, 120, 123, 139, 141, 148, 150, 171, 175–6
reincarnation 25, 48
Rembang, I Nyoman of Sesetan, Badung 11, 92
Renon village 105, 171, 175
repertoire 22, 26, 28, 37, 45, 48, 56, 62, 64–5, 84–112, 119–20, 151, 155–6
repetition(s) 47–8, 63, 81, 83, 85
resik 17
reyong *41*, 43–4, 49, 54, 59–60, *70*, 70, 75–6, 78–9, 81–2, 88, 90, 92, 97–9, 106, 115, 117, 141, 171, 176–8
reyong gongs 70
reyong kotekan 75, 78–9
rhythmic patterns 56, 107
Rintig, I Ketut 11
rindik (see *tingklik*) *45*, 45, 177–8
ritardandos 59
ritual Baris dancers, N. Bali *72*
romon 17
rontog 17
Roni, Ni Wayan 11
royal court music 98

S

sacred gamelan 103–6
Sadia, I Ketut of Binoh 94
Sadmertha village near Denpasar 90, 159
Salju (Snow), a composition 132
Sangkaragung village, Jemhrana 102
sangsih 54–6, 75–6, 78, 175–7
Sanskrit 110
Sanur village 100, 105

Sardono, Javanese choreographer 108
saron 39, *42*, 98, 105, 173, 177
Sawan village 33, 90
Sayan village 14, 20, 97, 121
Segah village, Karangasem 114–5
sekaha 116–7, 119–21, 124–6, 128–9,
137–8, 142, 177
Sekar Gendot, a compositon 95
sekaha pepaosan 110
Sekar Jaya (American group) 8, 10–1,
143–4, 156
Sekar Jepun (Japanese group) 143
Sekar Sungsang, a composition 95
sekar ageng 110
sekar alit 111
sekar madya 111
seledet *78*, 81, 177
selisir 37, 177
Semarandhana, a composition 104
semar pegulingan 28, 36–7, 92–4,
124, 156
Sempidi village near Denpasar 105
sendratari music/dance/drama form
129, 140, 177
shadow play(s) *(wayang kulit)* 30, 37,
65, 84, 95, 139, 173, 176
Sibang village near Denpasar 90, 157
Sidan village, Gianyar 98
Singapadu, Gianyar 34, 105, 112, 129
Singaraja 24, 44, 90, 104
Sinti, I Wayan 11, 94, 105, 111, 151
sisya 93, 177
slanketan 101, 177
slendro, 5-tone scale 36–8, 65, 95, 97,
99, 173, 177
sloka 110
solfége 17, 37
Solo, a composition 94
Spies, Walter (European painter) 20,
68, 108
Srinatih, Gusti Ayu 11
STSI (now ISI) 30, 174
Sudirana, Wayan, drummer 8, *12,* 154
Sujana, I Wayan 11
Sukarno, President 29

Sukawati village 24, 94, 96, 105
Sulahaan village 99, 151–2
suling (flutes) 24–25, 45, 49, 54, 59,
62, 81, 88, 97, 100, 109, 111, 126,
177
suling gambuh 45
suling kantilan 45
Sumandhi, 1 Nyoman, musician/danc-
er/puppeteer 9–11, 96
Suryatini, Ketut 11, 122, 158
sunaren 137, 177
Suta, I Madé 11
Suweca, I Wayan, drummer/lecturer
10, 11, 92, 121, 126, 156–60, *157*
Swasthi Bandem, Ni Luh 10
syncopation 53–6, 81

T
Tabanan village 88, 91, 96, 98, 101,
105
tabuh 16, 177
Tabuh-Tabuhan, a composition 20
tabuh kutus lelambatan pengawak
62–3
tabuh pisan lelambatan pengawak 62
taksu 121, 177
Tama, I Ketut 11
Tangkas, Klungkung 103, 105
tari lepas 88–9, 98, 119, 137, 173–4,
177
Taruna Gandrung 89
Taruna Jaya *12*, 89, 177
tawa-tawa 43, 97, 178
teachers 117–20
Tegalcangkering village, Jembrana
101–2
Teges Kanginan village 94, 96
Tegunungan, Gianyar 102
Tejakula 96
tekep 17
tektekan 108, 178
tembang 111–2, 178
Tembres, 1 Wayan, teacher 11, 92,
126–29, *127*
tembung 37*,* 178

tempo 48, 50, 55, 58–60, 63–4, 69, 71, 83, 115, 118, 128, 151, 160
Tenganan village 103–5
Terip, I Madé 92
Tihingan village, near Semarapura 33
tingklik/grantang/rindik 45, 45, 99–101, 140, 174, 177–8
Tirtha Sari group 94
Tista village 94
topeng 119, 178
tukang kendang 178
tourism and music 30–1
tour abroad 20, 149
trompong 41, 43, 49, 51–4, *53*, 62–3, 87, 88, 92–3, 98, 106, 159, 175, 178
trompong player *53, 87*
tukang 178
tuning systems 36–8
Tutur, I Ketut 11

U
Ubud 7, 30, 93, 102, 148–9, 154
UCLA 19, 21, 143
ugal 41, 71, 39, 51–4, 59–60, 70–1, 73–4, 76, 78, 81–2, 178
universities which maintain gamelans 143

V
venues for hearing music 138–40
village music 23
vocal music 109–12

W
wadon (female *kendang)* 44, 56, 76, 172, 174–5, 178
wayang kulit 95, 109–10, 178
wayang tantri 96
wayang wong 109
Wenten, I Nyoman 11
Wenten, Nanik 11
Wesleyan University 129
Widiantini, Putu 8, *12*
Wija, I Wayan, dalang 96
Windha, Nyoman, composer 11, 104, 115, 150
Wira, I Wayan 11
Wiratini, Ni Madé 11
wirama 110
women and music 122–4
women puppeteers 122

Contents of the Compact Disc

Track	Ensemble type	Performers from
1	Gamelan Gong Kebyar	STSI Academy, Kodya
2	Gamelan Gong Kebyar	STSI Academy
3	Gamelan Gong Kebyar	STSI Academy
4	Gamelan Gambuh	Pedungan, Badung
5	Gamelan Pelegongan	Binoh, Badung
6	Gamelan Gender Wayang	Padang Kertha, Karangasem
7	Gamelan Angklung	Mas, Gianyar
8	Gamelan Gong (Gdé)	Demulih, Bangli
9	Gamelan Joged Bumbung	Tegalcangkring, Jembrana
10	Gamelan Gandrung	Kesiman, Kodya
11	Gamelan Geguntangan (Tembang Arja)	Jero Suli (vocal) and musicians, Kodya
12	Gamelan Semaradana	Sanggar Çudamani musicians with Rachel Lowry, trumpet, and Colin MacDonald, saxophone

All music except selection 6 and 12 recorded by Michael Tenzer using a Sony TCD5M recorder with two Beyer microphones. Except for selections 3 and 5 composers or arrangers of these works are unknown to me, and most probably to the performers as well. In the course of preparing this CD I did not have opportunity to research this question further. Moreover I regret that I am unable to list the names of all of the many dozens of musicians performing on these recordings.

Composition title	Page references	Recording date	Time
Baris (demonstration)	60–62, 67–83, 161	July 12, 1989	5:06
Baris (perf. version).	67–83, 58–62	July 12, 1989	4:06
Jaya Semara (arr. Wayan Beratha, 1964)	87–92	July 12, 1989	3:51
Tabuh Gari	24–25, 36, 92	June 14, 1987	5:13
Solo (comp. Wayan Lotring, ca. 1920s)	28–29, 65–66, 92–94	Oct. 23, 1982	7:55
Embombuan	65, 94–96	March 1986, rec. Wayne Vitale	7:39
Pengecet Crucuk Punyah	65, 96–98	Oct. 25, 1982	4:14
Tabuh Telu Gdé	62–64, 98–99	Oct. 8, 1982	6:55
Camar Kilang (fragment)	64, 99–101	Aug. 3, 1987	5:13
Kembang Apak	102–103	Sept. 4, 1982	7:45
Sinom Tamtam	109–112	July 28, 1985	5:18
Arakok (comp. Wayan Sudirana, 2006)	153–155	July 11, 2006 **Total Time:**	7:13 **70:34**

Notes

1. This selection complements Chapter 5, which is devoted to an analysis of the Baris dance's opening ostinato. The various parts in the texture are presented individually and in small combinations, all at a slow tempo. The *gilak* gong pattern and steady beat of the *kempli* remain constant throughout. The other instruments are introduced in two different ways: first in the same order in which they are introduced in the chapter, each for four cycles, with one cycle of gilak alone separating entrances. At the end they come in once again in a "pyramid" from simplest to most complex part, adding a new layer with each cycle. The plan is as follows:

a. Introduction (*kendang* fanfare followed by full *gamelan*) →
b. gong, *kempur* and kempli →   **c.** *ugal* →
d. *gangsa (polos)*   →   **e.** gangsa *(sangsih)* →
f. ugal, gangsa (all)   →   **g.** *calung* →
h. *jegogan*   →   **i.** *reyong* (polos*)* →
j. reyong (sangsih)   →   **k.** reyong (all) →
l. *kendang wadon*   →   **m.** *kendang lanang* →
n. *kendang* (both)   →
o. "pyramid": jegogan, calung, ugal, gangsa, reyong and kendang →
p. ending.

2. Baris at performance speed, with the addition of *suling* (bamboo flute) and incorporation of *angsel*, dynamic and tempo changes linked to the choreography.
3. Jaya Semara (see p. 79) is a well-known composition from the early days of *kebyar* which opens with rapidly changing motives and textures but eventually settles on a repeating 16-beat melody.
4. Tabuh Gari is conventionally used as opening instrumental music for the *gambuh* theater. It comprises an opening *gineman* in unmeasured rhythm, followed by a slow-moving *pengawak* cycle and a brisker, concluding *pengecet*.
5. Solo was composed by Wayan Lotring, reputedly after returning to Bali from Surakarta (Solo), Central Java, where he and his gamelan performed for the Sultan.

6. Embombuan entwines interlocking figuration and melody, intricately split between polos and sangsih, and left and right hand parts.

7. Pengecet Crucuk Punyah uses a 48-beat melody with shifting figuration patterns, and an asymmetrically-structured introduction. Pengecet designates the animated tempo, *crucuk* is a type of bird, and *punyah* means "drunken".

8. Tabuh Telu Gdé uses the *tabuh telu* gong pattern, a 16-beat structure with the large gong sounding at the end of each cycle, the small kempli at the first and third quarter-way points, and the mid-sized kempur at two beats on either side of the kempli in the latter half of the cycle.

9. Camar Kilang reflects the influence of *gong kebyar* musical style on the bamboo *gamelan joged bumbung*. This fragment, from the opening of the composition, uses a melody adapted from the repertoire of the *gamelan gender wayang*.

10. Kembang Apak is an instrumental work probably introduced to the Kesiman musicians by their teacher Nyoman Kaler in the 1920s. It is similar in design to Lotring's music for the *gamelan pelegongan*; compare to track 5 above.

11. Sinom Tamtam is a setting of geguritan poetry in the *sekar alit* poetic meter known as *sinom* (p. 101). Each stanza has 10 lines, with the following syllable-counts and vowel-endings: 8-a, 8-i, 8-a, 8-i, 7/8-i, 8-u, 7/8-a, 8-1, 4-u, 8-a. Musicians in this small gamelan include Wayan Pogog (suling) and Wayan Saplug (kendang), renowned throughout South Bali during the 1950s, 60s and 70s.

12. Arakok demonstrates some of the most recent developments in Balinese music. Using instruments from the *gamelan semaradana* plus trumpet and alto saxophone, it includes multiple simultaneous melodies (counterpoint) irregular time structures (including one based around a meter of 31/16) and the full 7-tone *pélog* scale.

This CD contains <u>MP3 audio files.</u>

You can play MP3 files on your computer (most computers include a default MP3 player); in your portable MP3 player; on many mobile phones and PDAs; and on some newer CD and DVD players.

You can also convert the MP3 files and create a regular audio CD, using software and a CD writing drive.

To play your MP3 files:

1. Open the CD on your computer.
2. Click on the MP3 file that you wish to play, to open it. The file should start playing automatically. *(If it doesn't, then perhaps your computer does not have an MP3 player; you will need to download one. There are dozens of players available online, and most of them are free or shareware. You can type "mp3 player" or "music downloads" into your search engine to find some.)*